Better Homes and Gardens®

PORK, SAUSAGE & HAM

COOK BOOK

© 1979 by Meredith Corporation, Des Moines, Iowa.
All Rights Reserved. Printed in the United States of America.
First Edition. Fifth Printing, 1982.
Library of Congress Catalog Card Number: 78-74938
ISBN: 0-696-00055-5

On the cover: *Chops with Mushroom Sauce* served with hot, cooked noodles (see recipe, page 18), *Apricot-Wine Glazed Ham* (see recipe, page 51), and an array of sausages that vary in flavor, texture, and shape.

BETTER HOMES AND GARDENS® BOOKS

Editor-in-Chief: James A. Autry
Editorial Director: Neil Kuehnl
Executive Art Director: William J. Yates

Editor: Gerald M. Knox
Art Director: Ernest Shelton
Associate Art Directors: Randall Yontz,
    Neoma Alt West
Copy and Production Editors: David Kirchner,
    Lamont Olson, David A. Walsh
Assistant Art Director: Harijs Priekulis
Senior Graphic Designer: Faith Berven
Graphic Designers: Linda Ford,
    Rich Lewis, Sheryl Veenschoten,
    Tom Wegner
Food Editor: Doris Eby
Senior Associate Food Editor: Sharyl Heiken
Senior Food Editors: Sandra Granseth,
    Elizabeth Woolever
Associate Food Editors: Mary Cunningham,
    Joanne Johnson, Joy Taylor, Pat Teberg
Recipe Development Editor: Marion Viall
Test Kitchen Director: Sharon Golbert
Test Kitchen Home Economists: Jean Brekke,
    Kay Cargill, Marilyn Cornelius,
    Maryellen Krantz, Marge Steenson

Pork, Sausage, and Ham Cook Book

Editors: Sandra Granseth, Joy Taylor
Copy and Production Editor: David A. Walsh
Graphic Designer: Harijs Priekulis
Consultant: Max Cullen

Better Homes and Gardens
TEST KITCHEN®

Our seal assures you that every recipe in the *Pork, Sausage, and Ham Cook Book* is endorsed by the Better Homes and Gardens Test Kitchen. Each recipe is tested for family appeal, practicality, and deliciousness.

Contents

Facts About Pork

You will be inspired to serve pork more often, rather than just on special occasions, after acquainting yourself with *Better Homes and Gardens Pork, Sausage, and Ham Cook Book.* Because of improved technology in breeding and feeding, pork today is a high quality, lean meat. Pork is low in fat, and will add protein, vitamins, and iron to your diet.

In this book you'll find many delicious and tempting ways to prepare pork, sausage, and ham—whether you are a novice or an expert at preparing and cooking meat. In addition to the wide variety of recipes, we have included some grilling, microwave, and crockery cooking directions. Cook a pork roast or ham to perfection by following our basic roasting and baking charts. Also, throughout the cook book are illustrated tips that clarify meat cookery techniques. There's even a recipe collection of sauces, glazes, and marinades geared to bring out the best meat flavors. Turn to our handy, informational *Meat Guide* where you will find everything you need to know about buying and storing meat. Carve pork roasts and hams like a pro by following the easy-to-understand illustrations in this section.

Meat cuts can be confusing! To help you identify common pork and ham cuts and the various sausages, we've included color photographs and brief descriptions in each chapter. The photographs are especially helpful to compare the size and shape of the various meat cuts. Note the diagram at right which shows where the various meat cuts come from in the animal. Check these valuable sources when you're unfamiliar with a meat cut; next time you purchase meat you'll be a more-informed consumer.

Serve soups, stews, casseroles, sandwiches, salads, snacks, crepes, and more, and discover that pork has never been more delicious!

Retail Cuts

Shoulder

Arm Picnic
Smoked Picnic Whole
Arm Roast
Blade Boston Roast
Smoked Shoulder Roll
Blade Steak
Arm Steak
Cubed Steak
Pork Cubes
Ground Pork
Pork Hocks

Loin

Blade Roast
Center Loin Roast
Center Rib Roast
Rib Crown Roast
Boneless Top Loin Roast
Canadian-Style Bacon
Sirloin Roast
Tenderloin
Blade Chop
Rib Chop
Butterfly Chop
Loin Chop
Top Loin Chop
Sirloin Chop
Sirloin Cutlet
Back Ribs
Country-Style Ribs
Cubed Steak

Side

Fresh Side Pork
Spareribs
Slab Bacon
Salt Pork

Leg

Fully Cooked Ham
Cook-Before-Eating Ham
Canned Ham
Fresh Ham

Pork

Serve pork roasted, broiled, braised, or grilled, and you'll discover that it is tasty, nutritious, and better than ever. Count on versatile ground pork when your budget needs trimming, and treat your family to an elegant pork crown rib roast for that special occasion. Fill the gap between penny-wise and extravagant with the many other pork cuts such as shoulder and loin roasts, chops, steaks, and ribs. You'll find in this chapter tempting variations for pre-paring all cuts of pork, plus creative uses for leftovers. Fresh pork is most flavorful and juicy when cooked to an internal temp-erature of 170°. Cooking beyond 170°, as recommended years ago, results in dryness, less tenderness, and excessive shrinkage in the meat. Serve today's new, lean pork for mealtime variety that's low in calories and easy to digest, and for overall eating satisfaction.

Pork Identification

1 Loin Center Loin Roast
2 Loin Blade Roast
3 Loin Sirloin Roast
4 Loin Country-Style Ribs
5 Spareribs
6 Loin Back Ribs
7 Shoulder Arm Picnic
8 Shoulder Blade Boston Roast
9 Smoked Shoulder Picnic Whole
10 Shoulder Arm Roast
11 Smoked Shoulder Roll
12 Pork Shank

13 Boneless Loin Top Loin
    Roast
14 Shoulder Blade Steak
15 Tenderloin
16 Cubed Steak
17 Fresh Side Pork
18 Loin Chop
19 Loin Rib Chop
20 Loin Top Loin Chop
21 Loin Butterfly Chop
22 Smoked Loin Rib Chop
23 Pork Cubes

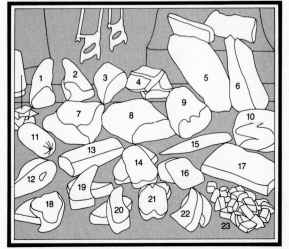

Identifying Pork

Pork Roasts

Shoulder Arm Picnic: (Also referred to as a fresh picnic.) The round arm bone identifies this roast, which is cut from the lower shoulder area. This roast contains the shank bone, and is less tender than the Shoulder Blade Boston Roast. May be sold boned, rolled, and tied. When cured and smoked it is labeled *Smoked Shoulder Picnic Whole* or smoked picnic. This smoked roast often is confused with a ham, which is from the hind leg. The smoked cut may be labeled "fully cooked" or "cook before eating."

Shoulder Arm Roast: A square-shaped roast from the upper portion of the Shoulder Arm Picnic. It contains the round arm bone; the shank has been removed.

Shoulder Blade Boston Roast: (Also referred to as a Boston butt roast or butt roast.) A square-shaped roast with identifying blade bone from the upper shoulder. It is sold boned, rolled, and tied, also. When cured and smoked, the boneless meat is called *Smoked Shoulder Roll*.

Loin Blade Roast: Includes the first 5 to 7 rib bones and may have the blade bone removed. The loin eye is the main muscle.

Loin Center Loin Roast: Cut between the Loin Blade Roast and the Loin Sirloin Roast. It includes a portion of the tenderloin.

Loin Center Rib Roast: A Center Loin Roast with the tenderloin removed. Two rib roasts tied together make a *Rib Crown Roast*.

Boneless Loin Top Loin Roast: A flat-shaped loin eye muscle. Two roasts may be tied together in a roll shape. When shaped into a compact roll, cured, and smoked, it's called *Canadian-Style Bacon*.

Loin Sirloin Roast: Cut from loin section nearest the leg. Contains backbone and hip bone. The largest muscle is the loin eye; the smaller muscle is the tenderloin.

Tenderloin: The small, tender, tapering muscle that extends through part of the loin. It usually weighs 1 pound or less.

Leg (Fresh Ham): From the hind leg. It comprises the rump portion, the center roast, and the shank portion. Also sold boned, rolled, and tied.

Pork Steaks and Chops

Shoulder Blade Steak: Cut from the Shoulder Blade Boston. It contains the blade bone.

Shoulder Arm Steak: Cut from the Shoulder Arm Picnic. It contains the round arm bone.

Cubed Steak: Any boneless piece of pork that has been put through a tenderizing machine.

Loin Blade Chop: Cut from the first 5 to 7 ribs. It may have the blade bone removed.

Loin Rib Chop: Contains the tender rib eye muscle, but no tenderloin. When cut thicker with a pocket, it's called *Loin Rib Chop for Stuffing*. When cured and smoked, it's called *Smoked Loin Rib Chop*.

Loin Butterfly Chop: A boneless chop that starts as a thick loin eye muscle split almost in half.

Loin Chop: Cut between the Loin Rib Chop and the Loin Sirloin Chop. It includes a portion of the tenderloin that is separated from the loin eye muscle by a T-shaped bone. When cured and smoked, it's called a *Smoked Loin Chop*.

Loin Top Loin Chop: Cut from the center loin section; the tenderloin has been removed. When cut 1¼ to 1½ inches thick, it's called an *Iowa Chop*.

Loin Sirloin Chop: (Also called sirloin steak.) Cut from the loin section nearest the hind leg. It contains a section of backbone and/or hip bone.

Loin Sirloin Cutlet: (Also called a cutlet.) Boneless, lean piece from the wedge-shaped area above the hip bone.

Other Pork Cuts

Loin Back Ribs: Contain rib bones from rib area of loin. The thicker layer of meat covering ribs comes from the loin eye. These often are smoked.

Loin Country-Style Ribs: The meatiest of all the pork ribs. They're cut from the front (shoulder) end of the back ribs, then split open.

Spareribs: Come from the rib cage. A thin covering of meat surrounds and attaches the ribs. A large portion of the weight is bone.

Ground Pork: Can be made from the less popular cuts of meat. Unseasoned.

Pork Cubes or pieces: (Also called boneless cubed pork.) Boneless, lean pieces cut from any meaty section.

Pork Hock: (Also called pork shank.) Mostly bone and cartilage with little meat. May be fresh, pickled, or cured and smoked. When cured and smoked, they're referred to as *Smoked Pork Hocks*.

Fresh Side Pork: The whole piece removed from the side. It may be sliced. It's called *Salt Pork* when salt is rubbed on the pieces. When cured and smoked, it's called *Slab Bacon,* which may be sliced.

Pork Jowl: Square piece in front of shoulder. It's often smoked and may be sliced.

Pigs Feet: May be fresh, smoked, or pickled.

Roasting Pork

Trim off excess fat from roast, leaving thin layer of fat over meat to protect lean portion from drying out. Sprinkle salt and pepper on fresh pork roasts. Place meat, fat side up, on rack in shallow roasting pan. Use an adjustable rack or a flat rack large enough to hold roast off bottom of pan. The rack may be omitted when roasting meat with rib bones because the rib bones serve as a rack.

Insert meat thermometer, placing thermometer so its bulb rests in center of the thickest portion of meat, and does not rest in fat or touch bone. Do not add water or other liquid, and do not cover the roasting pan.

Roast the meat in a 325° oven until meat thermometer registers the specified temperature. (To check temperature, push

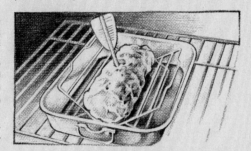

thermometer into meat a little farther.) For easier carving, let meat stand about 15 minutes. During this time, the meat will keep on cooking. Therefore, larger roasts should be removed when thermometer registers about 5° below the specified internal temperature. However, the thermometer should register the correct temperature when you carve the meat.

Use the roasting times given in the chart as a guide to total cooking time for the meat cut.

Pork Cut	Approximate Weight (pounds)	Internal Temperature of Meat	Approximate Cooking Time (total time)
	Roast meat at constant 325° oven temperature		
Shoulder Arm Picnic	5 to 8	170°	3 to 4 hours
Smoked Shoulder Picnic Whole			
cook-before-eating	5 to 8	170°	3 to 4½ hours
fully-cooked	5 to 8	140°	2½ to 3¼ hours
Shoulder Arm Roast	3 to 5	170°	2 to 3 hours
Shoulder Blade Boston Roast	4 to 6	170°	3 to 4 hours
Boneless Shoulder Blade			
Boston Roast	3 to 5	170°	2 to 3 hours
Smoked Shoulder Roll	2 to 3	170°	1¼ to 1¾ hours
Loin Blade Roast	3 to 4	170°	2¼ to 2¾ hours
Loin Center Loin Roast	3 to 5	170°	1¾ to 2½ hours
Loin Center Rib Roast	3 to 5	170°	1¾ to 2½ hours
Rib Crown Roast	4 to 6	170°	2¾ to 3½ hours
Boneless Loin Top			
Loin Roast (double)	3 to 5	170°	2 to 3 hours
Boneless Loin Top Loin Roast	2 to 4	170°	1¼ to 2 hours
Loin Sirloin Roast	3 to 5	170°	2¼ to 3¼ hours
Tenderloin	1	170°	¾ to 1 hour
Leg (fresh ham)	12 to 16	170°	5 to 6 hours
Leg (fresh ham), half	5 to 8	170°	3¼ to 4¾ hours

Pork Roasts

Roast Pork with Sprouts

- 1 3- to 4-pound pork roast
- 2 pints fresh brussels sprouts *or* two 10-ounce packages frozen brussels sprouts, thawed
- 2 medium onions, cut into thin wedges
- 2 tablespoons butter *or* margarine
- 2 teaspoons snipped fresh basil *or* ½ teaspoon dried basil, crushed
- ½ teaspoon salt
- ⅛ teaspoon pepper

Roast meat according to basic roasting directions on page 9. Just before roast is done, prepare vegetables. Trim stems of fresh brussels sprouts. Halve large sprouts. In covered saucepan combine brussels sprouts, onions, butter, basil, salt, and pepper. Cook, stirring occasionally, 8 to 10 minutes or till sprouts are tender. Serve vegetables with meat. Serves 6 to 8.

Apple-Stuffed Rib Roast

- 1 4-pound pork loin center rib roast, backbone loosened
- 1 20-ounce can sliced apples
- 1 pound ground pork
- 9 slices dry raisin bread, cut into ½-inch cubes
- 1 teaspoon ground cinnamon
- ¾ teaspoon salt
- ½ teaspoon ground cardamom
- ¼ teaspoon ground allspice
  Dash pepper

Place roast rib side down. Cut pockets in roast from meaty side between rib bones. Season with salt and pepper. Drain apples, reserving juice. Finely chop apples and set aside. Add water to reserved juice to make 1 cup liquid; set aside.

In skillet cook ground pork till browned; drain off excess fat. Stir in bread cubes, apples, cinnamon, salt, cardamom, allspice, and pepper. Add reserved apple liquid; toss to moisten. Spoon about ½ cup stuffing into each pocket of roast. (Spoon remaining stuffing into a 1-quart casserole; cover and refrigerate.) Place roast, rib side down, in shallow roasting pan. Insert meat thermometer in meat so it doesn't touch bone. Roast meat in 325° oven for 1½ hours or till meat begins to brown. Cover loosely with foil to prevent stuffing from overbrowning. Roast 1 to 1½ hours more or till meat thermometer registers 170°. Bake stuffing in casserole, uncovered, with roast the last 40 minutes of roasting. Serves 8.

Pork Crown Roast with Apricot Stuffing

- 1 5½- to 6-pound pork rib crown roast (12 to 16 ribs)
- 1 tablespoon sugar
- 1 teaspoon instant chicken bouillon granules
- ¾ cup hot water
- ¼ cup snipped dried apricots
- 4 cups dry whole wheat bread cubes (5½ slices bread)
- 1 large apple, peeled, cored, and chopped
- ½ teaspoon finely shredded orange peel
- ½ teaspoon salt
- ½ teaspoon ground sage
- ¼ teaspoon ground cinnamon
- ⅛ teaspoon pepper
- ½ cup chopped celery
- ¼ cup chopped onion
- ¼ cup butter *or* margarine
- ¼ cup orange juice
- 1 tablespoon light corn syrup
- ½ teaspoon soy sauce

Place roast, bone tips up, on rack in shallow roasting pan. Season with a little salt and pepper. Make a ball of foil and press into cavity to hold open. Wrap bone tips with foil. Insert meat thermometer, making sure bulb does not touch bone. Roast in 325° oven 2½ hours.

Meanwhile, prepare stuffing. Dissolve sugar and bouillon granules in hot water; pour over apricots. Let stand 5 minutes. In large bowl combine bread cubes, apple, orange peel, salt, sage, cinnamon, and pepper. Cook celery and onion in butter or margarine till tender; add to bread mixture. Add apricot mixture; toss lightly to moisten. (If desired, add ¼ cup additional water for a moister stuffing.)

Remove all foil from roast. Spoon stuffing lightly into center of roast, mounding high. Combine orange juice, corn syrup, and soy sauce; spoon some over meat. Roast, uncovered, 45 to 60 minutes more or till thermometer registers 170°; baste occasionally with orange juice mixture. Carefully transfer to warm platter. Garnish with canned apricot halves, if desired. Slice between ribs to serve. Serves 12 to 16.

Note: You may have to call ahead to your supermarket's meat department to place a special order for the crown roast. Make sure the fat is trimmed from the center of the roast.

Pork Crown Roast with Apricot Stuffing is an elegant entrée to feature at a special dinner party.

Roast Pork with Fennel

1 3- to 4-pound pork loin blade roast
½ teaspoon fennel seed
2 tablespoons sugar
1 teaspoon salt
1 teaspoon ground sage
1 teaspoon dried marjoram, crushed
¼ teaspoon celery seed
¼ teaspoon dry mustard
⅛ teaspoon pepper
1 tablespoon snipped parsley

Stud roast with fennel seed by inserting tip of knife into meat and pushing 4 or 5 seeds into a meat pocket as you remove knife. Cut about 15 evenly spaced pockets on meat's surface.

In a small bowl combine sugar, salt, sage, marjoram, celery seed, mustard, and pepper. Thoroughly rub the roast with sugar mixture. Cover roast; let stand 4 hours in the refrigerator.

Remove roast from refrigerator. Place meat on rack in shallow roasting pan. Insert meat thermometer. Roast, uncovered, in a 325° oven for 2¼ to 2¾ hours or till meat thermometer registers 170°. Remove from oven; place on warm serving platter. Sprinkle roast with parsley. Serves 8 to 10.

Glazed Pork Sirloin

1 4- to 5-pound pork loin sirloin roast
½ cup sugar
⅔ cup boiling water
⅓ cup vinegar
1 teaspoon hickory-smoked salt

Place roast on a rack in a shallow roasting pan. Insert meat thermometer. Roast, uncovered, in a 325° oven about 2 hours.

Meanwhile, in a small skillet heat and stir the sugar till a deep golden brown. Slowly stir in the boiling water. Stir in vinegar and hickory-smoked salt. Boil gently about 10 to 12 minutes or till mixture is reduced to ½ cup. (Mixture thickens with cooling.)

Brush pork with the sugar-vinegar mixture. Continue roasting about 30 minutes more or till meat thermometer registers 170°; brush often with sugar-vinegar mixture. Serves 10 to 12.

Note: Meat thermometer should register about 160° after the first 2-hour roasting time. Prepare sugar-vinegar mixture just before thermometer registers 160° so the mixture will still be warm when it's brushed on the roast.

Marinated Pork Roast

Marinade also is used in the gravy –

1 3- to 5-pound pork loin center loin roast
5 cloves garlic, halved
¼ cup cooking oil
¼ cup burgundy
¼ cup finely chopped onion
1 tablespoon worcestershire sauce
½ teaspoon dried thyme, crushed
½ teaspoon dried oregano, crushed
½ teaspoon celery salt
¼ teaspoon ground sage
¼ teaspoon pepper
Several dashes bottled hot pepper sauce
2 tablespoons all-purpose flour
1 teaspoon instant chicken bouillon granules

Stud roast with garlic halves by inserting tip of knife into meat and pushing cloves into a meat pocket as you remove knife. Make sure garlic is evenly spaced on meat's surface.

For marinade, in bowl combine oil, burgundy, onion, worcestershire sauce, thyme, oregano, celery salt, ground sage, pepper, and hot pepper sauce. Place meat in plastic bag; set in shallow baking dish. Pour marinade over meat; close bag. Marinate in refrigerator 6 to 8 hours or overnight, turning roast occasionally.

Drain the roast; reserve marinade. Place roast, rib side down, in shallow roasting pan. Insert meat thermometer. Roast, uncovered, in a 325° oven for 2½ to 3 hours or till thermometer registers 170°. Remove roast from oven and place on warm serving platter. Remove garlic clove halves from meat if possible.

To make gravy, pour off fat from the roasting pan. Return 2 tablespoons of the fat to the pan. Add the flour; stir to combine with the fat and to loosen meat particles. To reserved marinade add the chicken bouillon granules and enough water to make 1 cup liquid. Add all at once to the mixture in the roasting pan. Cook and stir till mixture is thickened and bubbly. Pass gravy with roast. Makes 6 to 8 servings.

Breaded Pork Tenderloin

- 1 **1-pound pork tenderloin, cut crosswise into 6 pieces**
- ⅓ **cup all-purpose flour**
- 1 **beaten egg**
- ¾ **cup fine dry bread crumbs (3 slices)**
- 2 **tablespoons finely chopped green onion**
- 3 **tablespoons cooking oil**

Pound pork pieces to ¼- to ⅛-inch thickness. Cut small slits around edges to prevent curling. Combine flour, ¼ teaspoon *salt,* and ⅛ teaspoon *pepper.* Combine egg and 1 tablespoon *water.* Combine bread crumbs and onion. Coat meat with flour mixture; dip in egg mixture, then in crumbs. In large skillet cook *half* the cutlets in hot oil 2 to 3 minutes on each side. Remove from pan to platter; keep warm. Add a little more oil if necessary. Repeat with remaining meat. Trim with lemon slices, if desired. Makes 6 servings.

Oriental-Style Tenderloin: Prepare as above *except* after pounding pork, place it in shallow baking dish. Stir together ¼ cup *dry sherry;* ¼ cup *soy sauce;* and 1 clove *garlic,* minced. Pour over pork and marinate at room temperature 30 minutes, turning pork twice; drain. Combine flour, salt, and pepper and continue as above.

Grilled Peachy Pork Roast

- 1 **teaspoon ground ginger**
- ½ **teaspoon dry mustard**
- 1 **4- to 5-pound boneless rolled pork loin top loin roast**
- 1 **16-ounce can peach slices**
- 2 **tablespoons lemon juice**
- 1 **tablespoon soy sauce**
- 1 **teaspoon worcestershire sauce**
- 1 **clove garlic, minced**

Combine ginger, mustard, 1 tablespoon *salt,* and ¼ teaspoon *pepper;* rub over roast. Insert spit rod through center of roast. Adjust holding forks; test balance. Insert meat thermometer near center of roast, not touching rod. Place *medium-hot* coals on both sides of drip pan. Attach spit; position drip pan under meat. Turn on motor. Grill 2 to 2½ hours or till thermometer registers 170°. Drain peaches, reserving ¼ cup syrup. In blender container mix peaches, reserved syrup, lemon juice, soy, worcestershire, and garlic. Cover; blend till smooth. During last 20 minutes of grilling, brush meat with sauce. Heat remaining sauce to pass. Serves 8 to 12.

Tenderloin Pinwheels

- 1 **1-pound pork tenderloin**
- 1½ **cups finely chopped fresh mushrooms**
- 2 **tablespoons butter *or* margarine**
- 1 **cup frozen peas, cooked and drained**
- 1 **beaten egg**
- 1 **cup soft bread crumbs (1¼ slices)**
- ½ **cup finely chopped fully cooked ham**
- ½ **teaspoon instant beef bouillon granules**

Split tenderloin lengthwise, cutting to, but not through, opposite side; open out flat. Working out from the center, pound tenderloin lightly with meat mallet to about a 10x6-inch rectangle. Sprinkle with a little salt. Cook mushrooms in *1 tablespoon* of the butter about 3 minutes or till tender; stir occasionally. Spread evenly over meat. Mash peas slightly with fork. Add egg, bread crumbs, ham, ¼ teaspoon *salt,* and dash *pepper.* Toss lightly. Spoon atop mushroom layer. Roll up jelly-roll style, beginning at narrow end. Tie meat with string, first at center, then at 1-inch intervals.

Place meat on rack in shallow roasting pan. Dissolve bouillon granules in ¼ cup *hot water.* Stir in remaining 1 tablespoon butter till melted. Brush some over meat. Roast, uncovered, in 325° oven about 1½ hours or till meat is tender; brush occasionally with remaining bouillon. Transfer meat to platter. Remove strings; slice. Serves 4.

Corned Pork Loin

- 1 **4- to 5-pound boneless pork loin top loin roast**
- 2 **tablespoons sugar**
- 2 **cloves garlic, minced**
- 2 **tablespoons mixed pickling spice**
- 2 **teaspoons minced dried onion**

Place meat in crock or large, deep, non-metal bowl. (Cut meat in half to make it fit, if necessary.) Dissolve sugar and ½ cup *salt* in 2 quarts *water.* Stir in remaining ingredients. Pour over meat. Cover meat with plate and weight it down to keep meat immersed. Refrigerate 10 days; turn meat occasionally. Drain off brine. Cover meat with water, and soak 1 to 2 hours. Drain; pat dry with paper toweling. Place meat on rack in shallow roasting pan. Insert meat thermometer. Roast, uncovered, in a 325° oven for 2 to 2½ hours or till thermometer registers 170°. Transfer meat to warm platter. Serves 12 to 15.

Pork Roast with Oriental Vegetables features a pork shoulder arm roast cooked in a soy sauce mixture.

Pork Roast with Oriental Vegetables

2 teaspoons grated gingerroot
2 tablespoons cooking oil
1 4-pound pork shoulder arm roast
2 cups water
1 large onion, coarsely chopped
¼ cup soy sauce
¼ cup red wine vinegar
2 tablespoons brown sugar
1 tablespoon instant chicken bouillon granules
1 teaspoon salt
½ teaspoon garlic powder
½ teaspoon pepper
4 cups fresh pea pods or two 6-ounce packages frozen pea pods, partially thawed
1 16-ounce can tomato wedges
1 8-ounce can water chestnuts, drained and sliced
1 cup sliced fresh mushrooms or one 3-ounce can sliced mushrooms, drained
¼ cup cold water
2 tablespoons cornstarch

In a large Dutch oven cook gingerroot in hot oil for 30 seconds. Add pork roast and brown meat on all sides in hot oil. Spoon off fat. Add the 2 cups water, the onion, soy sauce, vinegar, brown sugar, bouillon granules, salt, garlic powder, and pepper. Bring to boiling; reduce heat. Cover and simmer about 1½ hours or till tender.

Add pea pods, *undrained* tomatoes, water chestnuts, and mushrooms. Cover and simmer for 3 to 5 minutes more or till pea pods are crisp-tender. Remove meat and vegetables from Dutch oven; arrange on a warm platter. Keep warm.

Skim fat from juices; reserve 1¾ cups juices. Blend the ¼ cup cold water into the cornstarch; stir into the reserved juices. Cook and stir till mixture is thickened and bubbly. Serve vegetables and gravy with meat and hot, cooked *rice*. Makes 6 servings.

Pork Picnic with Apple-Curry Sauce

1 5- to 8-pound fresh pork shoulder arm picnic *or* smoked pork shoulder picnic whole (cook-before-eating)
Milk *or* light cream
2 teaspoons curry powder
2 tablespoons butter *or* margarine
2 medium apples, peeled, cored, and chopped (2 cups)
⅓ cup finely chopped onion
2 tablespoons all-purpose flour

Place meat on rack in shallow roasting pan. Insert meat thermometer. Roast in a 325° oven for 3 to 4 hours or till meat thermometer registers 170°. Remove meat, and place on serving platter; keep warm. Skim fat from pan juices; reserve no more than 2 tablespoons juices. Add milk or light cream to make 1 cup liquid; set aside.

In saucepan cook and stir curry powder in butter for 1 minute. Stir in apple and onion; cook, covered, till apple and onion are tender. Blend in flour. Add milk mixture all at once. Cook and stir over medium heat till thickened and bubbly.

Season sauce for fresh roast with salt and pepper to taste. If desired, spoon some sauce over roast. Pass remaining sauce with meat. Garnish platter with apple wedges and parsley sprigs, if desired. Makes 10 to 14 servings.

Apple-Glazed Boston Roast

1 4- to 6-pound pork shoulder blade Boston roast
1 14-ounce jar apple butter
⅓ cup beer
3 tablespoons brown sugar
¼ teaspoon ground cinnamon
⅛ teaspoon ground cloves

Place meat on rack in shallow roasting pan. Insert meat thermometer. Roast in 325° oven for 2 hours. Meanwhile, in a bowl stir together the apple butter, beer, brown sugar, cinnamon, and cloves. Spread apple butter mixture over top and sides of roast. Continue roasting for 1 to 2 hours more or till meat thermometer registers 170°. Heat any remaining apple butter mixture and pass with meat. Transfer roast to warm serving platter. Makes 10 to 12 servings.

Cider Pot Roast with Vegetables

- 2 cloves garlic, minced
- 2 tablespoons cooking oil
- 1 4-pound pork shoulder arm roast
- 2 cups apple cider *or* apple juice
- 3 medium onions, cut into thin wedges
- 2 teaspoons salt
- ¾ teaspoon dried tarragon, crushed
- ½ teaspoon pepper
- 2 bay leaves
- 3 large carrots, cut into 2-inch pieces
- 3 medium potatoes, peeled and quartered (1 pound)
- ½ small head cabbage, cut into wedges
- 2 cups small whole fresh mushrooms *or* one 8-ounce can whole mushrooms, drained
- 1 medium green pepper, cut into 1-inch squares
- ½ cup cold water
- ¼ cup all-purpose flour
- ½ teaspoon kitchen bouquet
  Salt
  Pepper
- 2 tablespoons snipped parsley

In a large Dutch oven cook garlic in hot oil for 30 seconds. Add pork roast, and brown meat in hot oil. Spoon off fat. Add apple cider or apple juice, onion wedges, salt, tarragon, pepper, and bay leaves. Bring to boiling; reduce heat. Cover and simmer for 1 hour or till meat is nearly tender.

Add carrots and potatoes. Cover and simmer for 15 minutes. Add cabbage wedges, mushrooms, and green pepper. Cook 15 minutes more or till meat and vegetables are tender. Remove meat and vegetables from Dutch oven; arrange on a warm platter. Keep warm.

Remove bay leaves; discard. Skim fat from juices; reserve 1¾ cups juices. (Add water if necessary; see note below.) Blend the cold water into the flour; stir into reserved juices. Cook and stir till thickened and bubbly. Stir in kitchen bouquet; simmer 2 to 3 minutes, stirring occasionally. Season to taste with salt and pepper. Serve vegetables and gravy with meat. Sprinkle meat and vegetables with snipped parsley before serving. Makes 6 to 8 servings.

Note: Because some pan lids don't fit as tightly as others and allow more evaporation, the amount of liquid remaining after cooking may vary. If too little liquid remains after cooking to use for the gravy, add water to the juices to total the amount of liquid specified.

Braised Pork Shanks

- 2 to 2½ pounds pork shanks, sawed into 2½-inch pieces (4 to 6 pieces)
- ¼ cup all-purpose flour
- ¼ cup olive oil *or* cooking oil
- 2 slices bacon, cut up
- 1 cup sliced carrot
- 1 cup chopped onion
- 2 cloves garlic, minced
- 1 16-ounce can tomatoes, cut up
- 1 cup dry red wine
- 1 cup beef broth
- ¼ cup snipped parsley
- 1 teaspoon dried savory, crushed
- ½ teaspoon dried basil, crushed
- ½ teaspoon dried oregano, crushed
- 1 bay leaf
- 2 tablespoons all-purpose flour

Coat meat with the ¼ cup flour. In Dutch oven brown shanks in hot oil. Remove; set aside. Cook and stir bacon, carrot, onion, and garlic in hot oil till bacon is crisp and vegetables are lightly browned. Drain off excess fat. Add shanks, tomatoes, wine, beef broth, parsley, savory, basil, oregano, bay leaf, and ½ teaspoon *salt*. Cover; bake in 325° for 1½ to 2 hours or till tender. Remove meat; keep warm. Remove bay leaf; discard. Skim fat from broth. Blend flour into ¼ cup cold *water;* stir into broth mixture. Cook and stir till thickened and bubbly. Arrange meat on hot, cooked *noodles*. Pour on some of the broth mixture; pass the remainder. Makes 4 servings.

Orange-Glazed Roll

- 1 2-pound smoked pork shoulder roll
- ¼ cup sugar
- 1 tablespoon cornstarch
- ¼ teaspoon ground allspice
- ½ cup orange juice
- ¼ cup honey
- ¼ cup butter *or* margarine
- 1 17-ounce can sweet potatoes, drained
- 1 orange, peeled and sectioned

Place shoulder roll on rack in shallow baking pan. Insert meat thermometer. Roast in 325° oven for 1 hour. Combine sugar, cornstarch, and allspice; blend in orange juice and honey. Cook and stir till thickened. Cook 1 minute more; stir in butter. Add sweet potatoes and orange sections to roast; spoon juice mixture over all. Roast about 30 minutes more or till meat thermometer registers 170°. Serves 8.

Pork Chops and Steaks

Basic Broiled Pork Chops and Steaks

Set the oven temperature to "broil" and preheat if desired (check range instruction booklet). Place meat on unheated rack of broiler pan. Broil pork 3 to 4 inches from heat for half the suggested time. Season with salt and pepper. Turn meat using tongs; cook till done. Season again. Use times in recipe or follow these as a guideline: pork rib or loin chops cut ¾ to 1 inch thick, 20 to 25 minutes total time; pork shoulder steaks cut ½ to ¾ inch thick, 20 to 22 minutes total time.

Basic Grilled Pork Chops and Steaks

Cook pork over *medium* coals till well done. A wire grill basket aids in turning chops.

Use times in recipes or follow these as a guideline. When cooking with a covered grill, allow 18 to 22 minutes total time for 1-inch-thick pork loin chops and 25 to 30 minutes for 1½-inch-thick loin chops. For an open grill, allow 22 to 25 minutes total time for the 1-inch-thick chops and 30 to 35 minutes for the 1½-inch-thick pork loin chops.

When grilling pork shoulder blade steaks cut ¾ inch thick, allow 15 to 20 minutes total time for both covered and open grills.

Crisp-Fried Pork Chops

```
  4  pork chops, cut ½ inch thick
  ¼  cup all-purpose flour
  ½  teaspoon salt
  ⅛  teaspoon pepper
  1  beaten egg
  1  teaspoon cooking oil
1½  cups soft bread crumbs (2 slices)
  3  tablespoons cooking oil
```

Coat chops with a mixture of flour, salt, and pepper; shake off excess flour. In bowl combine egg and 1 teaspoon oil. Dip chops in egg mixture; place in bread crumbs, patting crumbs onto meat. Arrange chops between pieces of waxed paper and refrigerate 30 to 60 minutes. In large, heavy skillet heat 3 tablespoons oil. Add breaded chops. Cook over medium-low heat about 40 minutes, turning occasionally. Add more oil, if necessary. Season to taste. Serves 4.

Stuffing Pork Chops

A

B

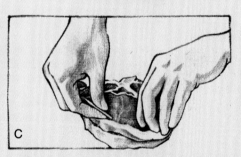

C

(A) To make a pocket in thick pork chops for stuffing, first cut a 1½- to 2-inch-long slit in the fatty side of the chop, using a sharp knife. Then, insert the knife into the slit and draw it from side to side to form a larger pocket inside the chop, cutting almost to bone edge. Try not to make the first slit any larger so that closing the chop will be easier.

(B) Use a spoon to stuff the chops. Divide stuffing mixture evenly among the chops and fill pockets lightly.

(C) To ensure that the stuffing stays in the pork chop pockets during baking, securely close the opening with one or two wooden picks inserted into the chops diagonally. Be sure to remove the wooden picks before serving the chops.

Chops with Mushroom Sauce

Broiled chops served on a bed of noodles mixed with green onion. Shown on the cover –

- **4 pork loin chops, cut 1¼ to 1½ inches thick (about 2¾ pounds)**
- **4 ounces medium noodles (3 cups)**
- **2 tablespoons butter *or* margarine**
- **1½ cups sliced fresh mushrooms**
- **2 tablespoons all-purpose flour**
- **1 cup chicken broth**
- **2 tablespoons snipped parsley**
- **1 teaspoon lemon juice**
- **1 slightly beaten egg yolk**
- **3 tablespoons milk**
- **¼ teaspoon salt**
- **Dash pepper**
- **½ cup sliced green onion**
- **2 tablespoons butter *or* margarine**

Place chops on unheated rack of broiler pan. Broil chops 5 inches from heat about 16 minutes. Sprinkle chops lightly with salt and pepper, if desired. Turn chops and broil about 16 minutes more or till chops are done.

Meanwhile, cook noodles according to package directions and prepare the mushroom sauce. For mushroom sauce, in saucepan melt 2 tablespoons butter or margarine. Add the sliced mushrooms; cook over medium-high heat about 5 minutes or till mushrooms are tender. Blend in flour. Add chicken broth. Cook, stirring constantly, till mixture is thickened and bubbly. Cook and stir 2 minutes more. Add the snipped parsley and lemon juice. Combine the slightly beaten egg yolk and milk; stir egg yolk mixture into mushroom sauce. Add the salt and pepper. Cook and stir over low heat 2 minutes more.

In small saucepan cook sliced green onion in the 2 tablespoons butter or margarine till onion is tender. Toss drained hot noodles with the butter-onion mixture. Arrange noodles on warm serving platter. Place the broiled chops atop the noodles. Spoon some of the mushroom sauce over chops. Pass the remaining mushroom sauce. Garnish platter with sprigs of parsley, if desired. Makes 4 servings.

Pineapple-Stuffed Chops

- **4 pork loin rib chops, cut 1 inch thick**
- **1 8-ounce can pineapple slices (juice pack)**
- **¼ cup catsup**
- **1 tablespoon sliced green onion**
- **1 tablespoon butter *or* margarine**
- **½ teaspoon dry mustard**

Cut pocket in each chop by cutting from fat side almost to bone edge. Season cavity with a little salt and pepper. Drain pineapple, reserving juice. Halve two slices of pineapple; cut up remaining pineapple and set aside. Place a pineapple half-slice in pocket of each chop, round side out. Grill chops over *medium* coals on covered grill about 20 minutes turning once.

Meanwhile, in small saucepan combine catsup, green onion, butter or margarine, dry mustard, and the reserved pineapple and pineapple juice. Heat to boiling; reduce heat and simmer 10 minutes. Grill chops 5 minutes more or till done, brushing with sauce. Spoon remaining sauce on chops before serving. Serves 4.

Grilled Rice-Stuffed Pork Chops

- **½ cup cold water**
- **¼ cup long grain rice**
- **1 teaspoon instant chicken bouillon granules**
- **½ teaspoon dry mustard**
- **¼ teaspoon ground sage**
- **¼ teaspoon salt**
- **¼ teaspoon pepper**
- **2 tablespoons chopped green onion**
- **1 2-ounce can chopped mushrooms, drained**
- **4 pork loin rib chops, cut 1 inch thick**

In saucepan combine cold water, rice, bouillon granules, mustard, sage, salt, and pepper; cover with tight-fitting lid. Bring to boiling; reduce heat. Simmer 10 minutes (do not lift cover). Remove from heat; let stand, covered, 10 minutes. Stir in green onion and mushrooms.

Cut pocket in each chop by cutting from fat side almost to bone edge. Season cavity with a little salt and pepper. Spoon about ¼ cup rice mixture into each pocket. Securely fasten pocket opening with wooden picks. Grill chops over *medium* coals 20 minutes; turn and grill about 10 minutes more. Before serving, remove the picks. Makes 4 servings.

You need only a few ingredients to prepare Pineapple-Stuffed Chops cooked on the barbecue grill.

Braised Pork Steaks

4 pork shoulder blade steaks, cut ½ inch thick (2½ to 3 pounds)
½ cup tomato sauce
¼ teaspoon ground sage

Trim excess fat from steaks; in large skillet cook fat trimmings till 2 tablespoons fat accumulate. Discard trimmings. Brown two steaks slowly on each side in hot fat; remove steaks. Repeat with remaining two steaks. Drain off excess fat. Return all steaks to skillet. Season with salt and pepper. Add tomato sauce and sage. Cover tightly; cook over low heat for 30 to 35 minutes or till meat is tender. Skim excess fat from juices. If necessary, cook down juices to thicken slightly; spoon over meat. Serves 4.

Oven Pork Steaks Dinner

4 pork shoulder steaks, cut ½ inch thick (2½ to 3 pounds)
2 tablespoons all-purpose flour
½ teaspoon salt
¼ teaspoon pepper
½ cup water
¼ cup dry white wine
1 tablespoon brown sugar
½ teaspoon ground sage
1 bay leaf
4 medium potatoes, peeled and quartered
4 medium carrots, quartered
2 medium onions, quartered
1 tablespoon cold water
2 teaspoons all-purpose flour
  Parsley

Trim excess fat from steaks. Combine 2 tablespoons flour, salt, and pepper; coat steaks with flour mixture. In an oven-going Dutch oven cook fat trimmings till about 2 tablespoons fat accumulate; discard trimmings. Brown the steaks, two at a time, in hot fat. Drain off excess fat; return all meat to pan. Add ½ cup water, wine, brown sugar, ground sage, and bay leaf.

Stir in potatoes, carrots, and onions. Bake, covered, in a 350° oven for 70 minutes or till meat and vegetables are tender. Remove bay leaf.

Transfer meat and vegetables to warm platter; keep warm. Skim fat from juices. Blend 1 tablespoon cold water into 2 teaspoons flour; stir into juices in Dutch oven. Cook and stir till thickened and bubbly. Spoon over meat and vegetables. Garnish with parsley. Serves 4.

Pork Paprikash

3 tablespoons all-purpose flour
1 tablespoon paprika
½ teaspoon salt
6 pork loin butterfly chops, cut ¾ inch thick
2 tablespoons cooking oil
½ cup chopped onion
¼ cup water
½ cup milk
4 teaspoons all-purpose flour
½ cup dairy sour cream

Combine the 3 tablespoons flour, the paprika, and salt; coat chops with flour mixture. In large skillet brown chops on both sides in hot oil. Add onion and water; cover and simmer over low heat for 30 to 45 minutes or till tender. Remove meat to platter; keep warm. Skim excess fat from pan juices. Blend the milk into the 4 teaspoons flour. Stir into pan juices. Cook and stir till thickened and bubbly. Stir in sour cream; heat through but *do not boil*. Arrange pork chops atop hot, cooked *noodles*. Spoon sauce over top. Sprinkle with additional paprika, if desired. Serves 6.

Pork and Rice a l'Orange

4 pork chops, cut ¾ inch thick (about 1½ pounds)
⅔ cup long grain rice
1 cup water
1 cup orange juice
½ cup chopped apple
¼ cup raisins
2 tablespoons brown sugar
½ teaspoon salt
¼ teaspoon ground cinnamon
  Thin orange slices (optional)

Trim excess fat from chops; in skillet cook fat trimmings till 2 tablespoons fat accumulate. Discard trimmings. Season chops with salt and pepper. Brown chops slowly in hot fat. Remove chops and set aside; reserve drippings. In same skillet cook rice in reserved drippings till golden, stirring constantly. Stir in water and orange juice; bring to boiling. Stir in apple, raisins, brown sugar, salt, and cinnamon. Turn mixture into a 9x9x2-inch baking pan. Arrange chops atop. Bake, covered, in a 350° oven for 40 minutes. Remove cover. Arrange orange slices atop, if desired. Bake, uncovered, 10 minutes more or till chops are tender. Makes 4 servings.

Oriental Chops and Rice

4 **pork chops, cut ½ inch thick**
2 **beaten eggs**
1 **2-ounce can chopped mushrooms**
⅔ **cup long grain rice**
¼ **cup sliced green onion**
¼ **cup chopped water chestnuts**
2 **tablespoons cooking oil**
2 **tablespoons soy sauce**
½ **teaspoon instant chicken bouillon granules**

Trim excess fat from chops; in skillet cook fat trimmings till 2 tablespoons fat accumulate. Discard trimmings. Brown chops in hot fat. Season with salt and pepper. Set chops aside; reserve drippings. Combine eggs and 2 tablespoons *water*. Cook eggs in reserved drippings in skillet till set. Invert skillet over baking sheet to remove cooked eggs in one piece. Cut eggs into narrow strips. Drain mushrooms. In same skillet cook mushrooms, rice, onion, and water chestnuts in hot oil till rice is golden; stir constantly. Stir in soy, bouillon granules, and 1¾ cups *water*. Bring to boiling. Remove from heat; stir in egg strips. Turn mixture into a 2-quart casserole. Arrange chops atop rice mixture. Sprinkle with paprika, if desired. Bake, covered, in 350° oven about 35 minutes or till chops and rice are tender. Remove chops; stir rice. Makes 4 servings.

Hawaiian Smoked Chops

1 **11-ounce can mandarin orange sections**
1 **8-ounce can pineapple chunks (juice pack)**
⅓ **cup chopped green pepper**
½ **teaspoon instant beef bouillon granules**
½ **teaspoon ground ginger**
1 **cup long grain rice**
¼ **cup apricot preserves**
4 **fully cooked smoked pork loin rib chops, cut ½ inch thick**

Drain fruits; reserve liquids (about 1 cup). Combine liquids and water to make 2¼ cups liquid. In skillet combine liquid, green pepper, bouillon granules, ginger, and 1 teaspoon *salt*. Stir in rice. Bring to boiling; cover and simmer 15 minutes. Stir in preserves, orange sections, and pineapple. Place chops on top. Cover; simmer 10 to 15 minutes more or till rice is tender and chops are heated through. Place chops on platter. Spoon rice mixture around chops. Makes 4 servings.

Saucy Tomato Chops

6 **pork chops, cut ½ inch thick**
2 **tablespoons cooking oil**
½ **cup chopped onion**
1 **clove garlic, minced**
1 **16-ounce can tomatoes**
1 **8-ounce can tomato sauce**
¼ **cup chopped green pepper**
1 **4-ounce can whole mushrooms, drained**
1 **teaspoon instant chicken bouillon granules**
¼ **teaspoon dried thyme, crushed**
3 **tablespoons all-purpose flour**

In large skillet brown chops on both sides in hot oil. Remove chops from skillet. Cook onion and garlic in drippings till onion is tender but not brown. Drain off excess fat.

Meanwhile, drain and cut up tomatoes, reserving ⅓ cup juice. To skillet add tomatoes, tomato sauce, green pepper, mushrooms, bouillon granules, and thyme. Bring to boiling. Arrange chops atop tomato mixture. Cover and simmer about 20 minutes, stirring occasionally. Remove cover; simmer 10 minutes more. Remove chops to platter; keep warm. Blend reserved tomato juice into flour. Stir into skillet; cook and stir till thickened and bubbly. Spoon over chops. Serve with hot, cooked *rice*. Makes 6 servings.

Crockery cooker directions: Brown chops; drain and cut up tomatoes as above. In electric slow crockery cooker combine onion, garlic, drained tomatoes, tomato sauce, green pepper, mushrooms, bouillon granules, and thyme. Place browned chops atop tomato mixture. Cover and cook on low heat setting for 4 to 5 hours. Place chops on a warm platter; keep warm. Turn cooker to high; blend reserved tomato juice into flour. Stir flour mixture into cooker. Cook and stir till thickened and bubbly. Pour some of the tomato mixture over chops; pass the remaining sauce. Serve with *rice*. Makes 6 servings.

Fat for Browning Chops

Use fat trimmed from the chops for browning. Heat trimmings in skillet until desired amount of melted fat accumulates, then discard trimmings. If there's not enough fat on meat, use shortening or cooking oil to make up the difference.

Arrange browned pork loin chops atop a rice-and-vegetable mixture for Mexicali Pork Chops.

Mexicali Pork Chops

  4 pork loin chops, cut ¾ inch thick (1¾ to 2
      pounds)
 ½ cup chopped green pepper
 ¼ cup chopped onion
  1 16-ounce can tomatoes, cut up
  1 8-ounce can whole kernel corn, drained
  1 8-ounce can red kidney beans, drained
 ½ cup long grain rice
 ½ cup water
  1 4-ounce can mild green chili peppers,
      rinsed, seeded, and chopped
 ¾ teaspoon salt
      Few dashes bottled hot pepper sauce

Trim excess fat from chops; in skillet cook fat trimmings till 2 tablespoons fat accumulate. Discard trimmings. Brown chops on both sides in hot fat. Season with salt and pepper. Set chops aside; reserve drippings in skillet. Cook green pepper and onion in reserved drippings till tender but not brown. Stir in *undrained* tomatoes, drained corn, drained kidney beans, uncooked rice, water, chili peppers, salt, and hot pepper sauce. Bring to boiling. Turn mixture into a 12x7½x2-inch baking dish. Arrange pork chops atop. Cover and bake in a 350° oven for 35 minutes. Uncover and bake 10 to 15 minutes more or till meat is tender. If desired, garnish with parsley. Makes 4 servings.

Pepper Chops

  2 tablespoons all-purpose flour
  6 pork loin rib chops, cut ¾ inch thick
  1 tablespoon cooking oil
  1 10½-ounce can condensed beef broth
 ½ cup chopped onion
 ½ cup chopped green pepper
  2 tablespoons vinegar
  2 tablespoons capers
  2 tablespoons all-purpose flour

Combine 2 tablespoons flour, ½ teaspoon *salt,* and dash *pepper;* coat chops. In large skillet brown chops on each side in hot oil. Add ¾ *cup* of the beef broth, the onion, green pepper, vinegar, and capers. Cover and simmer about 35 to 40 minutes or till tender. Remove chops to platter; keep warm. Add water to remaining beef broth to equal ¾ cup liquid. Blend into the remaining 2 tablespoons flour; add to skillet mixture. Cook and stir till thickened and bubbly. Serve chops with hot, cooked *rice;* pass gravy. Serves 6.

Fruit-Stuffed Pork Chops

  6 pork loin rib chops, cut 1½ inches thick
 ½ cup chopped celery
  1 medium apple, chopped (½ cup)
  2 tablespoons butter *or* margarine
  1 beaten egg
1½ cups toasted raisin bread cubes (2½
      slices bread)
 ½ teaspoon finely shredded orange peel
  1 orange, sectioned and chopped (⅓ cup)
 ¼ teaspoon salt
 ⅛ teaspoon ground cinnamon

Cut pocket in each chop by cutting from fat side almost to bone edge. Season cavity with a little salt and pepper. In small saucepan cook celery and apple in butter till tender but not brown. Combine egg, bread, orange peel, chopped orange, salt, and cinnamon. Pour cooked celery-apple mixture over bread cube mixture; toss lightly. Spoon about ¼ cup stuffing into each pork chop. Securely fasten pocket opening with wooden picks. Grill chops over *medium* coals about 20 minutes. Turn meat and grill 15 to 20 minutes or till done.

   Or, in large oven-going skillet brown stuffed chops slowly in hot *cooking oil* about 10 to 15 minutes. Drain off excess fat. Bake, uncovered, in a 350° oven for 45 to 60 minutes or till done.

   Before serving, remove picks. Garnish with orange slices, if desired. Makes 6 servings.

Chop and Kraut Skillet

  4 pork chops, cut ½ inch thick
  1 medium onion, sliced
  1 16-ounce can sauerkraut, drained and
      rinsed
  1 12-ounce can beer
  2 tablespoons brown sugar
  2 tablespoons chopped pimiento
  1 teaspoon caraway seed

Trim excess fat from chops; in skillet cook fat trimmings till about 2 tablespoons fat accumulate. Discard trimmings. Brown the chops and onion in hot fat. Remove chops from skillet. In skillet with onions, combine sauerkraut, beer, brown sugar, pimiento, and caraway seed. Simmer 5 minutes. Place chops atop; season with salt and pepper. Cover and simmer about 30 minutes; uncover and simmer 5 minutes more or till chops are tender. Makes 4 servings.

Stir-Fried Pork and Rice

3 **slightly beaten eggs**
3 **tablespoons cooking oil**
1 **pound pork cubed steaks, cut into**
   ½- to ¾-inch strips
1 **medium cucumber, thinly sliced**
1 **cup bias-sliced celery**
¼ **cup chopped green onion**
1 **small clove garlic, minced**
2 **cups cooked brown** *or* **long grain rice**
¼ **cup soy sauce**
2 **medium tomatoes, each cut into eighths**

In large skillet cook eggs in *1 tablespoon* of the oil till set, stirring just enough to break eggs into bite-size pieces; remove from skillet and set aside. In same skillet heat 1 tablespoon of the remaining oil. Cook meat strips, half at a time, till browned; remove from skillet and set aside. In same skillet cook and stir cucumber, celery, green onion, and garlic in remaining oil over medium-high heat about 4 minutes or till tender. Stir in cooked rice, soy sauce, browned pork, and cooked eggs. Arrange tomatoes on top; cover and cook about 3 minutes or just till tomatoes are hot. Pass additional soy sauce, if desired. Makes 4 servings.

Pork Rolls and Kraut

6 **pork cubed steaks, cut ¼ inch thick**
   (about 2 pounds)
6 **smoked sausage links**
2 **tablespoons cooking oil**
1 **7½-ounce can tomatoes, cut up**
⅓ **cup chopped onion**
1 **teaspoon caraway seed**
¼ **teaspoon dried thyme, crushed**
1 **8-ounce can sauerkraut**
¼ **cup cold water**
1 **tablespoon all-purpose flour**

Season cubed steaks with salt and pepper. Wrap meat around sausage links and secure with wooden picks. In large skillet brown meat rolls in hot oil; drain. Add *undrained* tomatoes, onion, caraway, and thyme. Cover and simmer about 20 minutes. Drain sauerkraut and add to skillet. Cook 5 minutes. Remove meat; discard picks. Blend water into flour; stir into mixture in skillet. Cook and stir till thickened and bubbly. Serve sauerkraut-tomato mixture over meat. Makes 6 servings.

Apple-Stuffed Pork Rolls

Stuff cubed steaks using a bread crumb mixture that includes raisins, onion, and shredded apple. Either bake in the oven or cook in a pressure cooker –

1½ **cups soft bread crumbs**
   (2 slices bread)
1½ **cups coarsely shredded, peeled apple**
½ **cup raisins**
2 **tablespoons chopped onion**
½ **teaspoon salt**
6 **pork cubed steaks, cut ¼ inch thick**
   (about 2 pounds)
2 **tablespoons cooking oil**
½ **teaspoon dried thyme, crushed**
1 **10½-ounce can condensed beef broth**
2 **tablespoons all-purpose flour**

Combine the bread crumbs, shredded apple, raisins, onion, and salt. Place equal portions of mixture atop the cubed steaks. Roll a cubed steak around each portion of filling; secure with string or wooden picks.

In skillet slowly brown meat on all sides in hot oil. Transfer meat rolls to 12x7½x2-inch baking dish. Add thyme to ⅔ *cup* of the broth; pour over meat. Cover and bake in a 350° oven for 30 minutes. Uncover; bake 10 minutes more or till meat is tender. Lift meat rolls onto serving platter; remove strings or wooden picks. Keep meat rolls warm while preparing gravy.

Skim fat from pan juices. Blend remaining beef broth into flour. Add to pan juices in saucepan. Cook and stir over low heat till thickened and bubbly. Spoon some of the gravy over pork rolls; pass the remaining gravy. Serves 6.

Pressure cooker directions: Prepare stuffing mixture and stuff the cubed steaks as above; tie with string. Omit browning of rolls in oil. In 4-quart pressure cooker add thyme to *1 cup* of the beef broth. Place pork rolls on a rack in the pressure cooker. Close cover securely. Cook at 15 pounds pressure for 10 minutes. Cool quickly under cold running water. Lift rolls onto serving platter; remove strings. Keep warm. Skim fat from pan juices. Blend the remaining beef broth into *3 tablespoons all-purpose flour*. Add to pan juices in cooker. Cook and stir till thickened and bubbly. Spoon some of the gravy over pork rolls; pass remaining gravy with meat.

Pork Ribs

Apricot-Glazed Spareribs

4 pounds meaty pork spareribs *or* pork loin
   back ribs, cut into serving-size pieces
¼ cup dried apricots
3 tablespoons frozen orange juice
   concentrate, thawed
2 tablespoons brown sugar
2 tablespoons hot-style catsup
1 teaspoon vinegar
½ teaspoon worcestershire sauce
¼ teaspoon dry mustard

Sprinkle ribs lightly with salt. Place, meaty side
down, in shallow roasting pan. Roast in 450°
oven for 30 minutes. Remove meat from oven;
drain off fat. Turn ribs, meaty side up. Reduce
oven temperature to 350°. Roast ribs 30 minutes
more. Meanwhile, place apricots in small
saucepan; add ⅔ cup *water*. Cover and simmer
15 to 20 minutes or till tender. Place apricot-
water mixture in blender container; cover and
blend till smooth. Add orange juice concentrate,
brown sugar, catsup, vinegar, worcestershire,
and dry mustard to blender. Process till smooth.
Drain fat from ribs. Brush ribs with some sauce.
Continue to roast 30 minutes more, brushing occasionally with remaining sauce. Makes 4 or 5
servings.

Oven-Baked Ribs and Kraut

3 pounds pork loin back ribs, cut into 2-rib
   portions
1 27-ounce can *or* two 16-ounce cans
   sauerkraut, drained
3 medium potatoes, peeled and sliced
⅓ cup chicken broth
1 2-ounce can (¼ cup) sliced pimiento,
   drained and chopped
½ teaspoon celery seed
1 medium onion, sliced and separated into
   rings
½ cup bottled barbecue sauce

Place ribs, meaty side down, in shallow roasting
pan. Roast in 450° oven for 20 minutes. Remove
meat from oven; drain off excess fat. Reduce
oven temperature to 350°. Combine the sauerkraut, potatoes, chicken broth, pimiento, and
celery seed. Place in the bottom of 13x9x2-inch
baking dish. Arrange onion rings atop. Place
ribs, meaty side up, in center of dish; sprinkle
with some salt. Brush barbecue sauce over ribs.
Cover and bake in 350° oven for 1½ to 1¾ hours
or till meat is tender. Makes 4 servings.

Ribs with Caper Sauce

2 to 2½ pounds meaty pork spareribs,
   sawed in half across bones
2 leeks, sliced (1½ cups)
1 cup dry white wine
⅓ cup snipped cilantro *or* parsley
¼ cup capers, drained if desired
2 cloves garlic, minced
1 teaspoon dried thyme, crushed
1 teaspoon ground sage
2 tablespoons cold water
1 tablespoon cornstarch

In a large saucepan or Dutch oven add enough
water to ribs to cover. Bring to boiling; reduce
heat. Cover and simmer for 45 minutes. Drain
well. Place ribs, meaty side up, in shallow roasting pan. Roast, uncovered, in 350° oven about
30 minutes. Meanwhile, in small saucepan
combine leeks, wine, cilantro or parsley, capers,
garlic, thyme, and sage. Cover and simmer
about 5 minutes. Slowly blend the 2 tablespoons
cold water into cornstarch. Stir into hot mixture.
Cook and stir till thickened and bubbly. Transfer
ribs to a warm platter. Pour sauce over ribs.
Garnish platter with sprigs of cilantro or parsley,
if desired. Makes 3 or 4 servings.

Spanish Spareribs

8 ounces pork sausage links
2½ to 3 pounds meaty pork spareribs, cut
   into 2-rib portions
3 slices bacon, cut up
½ cup chopped onion
1 clove garlic, minced
1 16-ounce can tomatoes
1 10½-ounce can condensed beef broth
½ cup sliced pimiento-stuffed olives
2 tablespoons snipped parsley
½ cup cold water
¼ cup all-purpose flour

In Dutch oven brown sausage links. Remove;
drain off fat. In same pan brown ribs, half at a
time; remove. Add bacon, onion, and garlic;
cook till bacon is crisp and onion is tender. Return meats to pan. Add *undrained* tomatoes,
beef broth, olives, and parsley. Cover and simmer 1 hour or till ribs are tender. Remove meats;
keep warm. Skim off fat; measure sauce. Add
water, if necessary, to make 2½ cups liquid; return to pan. Blend water into flour; stir into liquid.
Cook and stir till bubbly. Serve meat over
hot, cooked *noodles*. Pass sauce. Serves 6.

Pineapple Hawaiian Ribs and Sauced Country-Style Ribs are sure to tempt all rib-lovers.

Sauced Country-Style Ribs

    4 pounds pork loin country-style ribs
    ½ cup catsup
    ¼ cup water
    ¼ cup finely chopped onion
    3 tablespoons wine vinegar
    1 tablespoon cooking oil
    1 tablespoon brown sugar
    2 teaspoons worcestershire sauce
 1½ teaspoons whole mustard seed
    1 teaspoon paprika
    ½ teaspoon dried oregano, crushed
    ½ teaspoon chili powder
    ⅛ teaspoon ground cloves
    1 bay leaf
    1 clove garlic, minced

In large Dutch oven add enough water to ribs to cover. Bring to boiling; reduce heat. Cover; simmer 45 minutes. Drain. In saucepan combine remaining ingredients and ¼ teaspoon *salt*. Bring to boiling; simmer, uncovered, for 10 minutes, stirring once or twice. Discard bay leaf. Place ribs, meaty side up, in shallow roasting pan. Brush ribs generously with sauce. Roast, uncovered, in a 350° oven about 15 minutes. Brush with additional sauce. Roast 15 minutes more, brushing occasionally with sauce. Serve ribs with remaining heated sauce. Serves 4 to 6.

Portuguese Marinated Ribs

    1 cup water
    ¾ cup vinegar
    ½ teaspoon finely shredded lemon peel
    3 tablespoons lemon juice
    1 clove garlic, minced
    1 dried red chili pepper, seeded and
        crushed
    1 teaspoon ground cumin
    1 teaspoon salt
    ¼ teaspoon pepper
    4 pounds meaty pork spareribs, cut into
        serving-size pieces

Place large plastic bag in large bowl. In bag combine all ingredients except ribs; mix well. Add ribs; close bag tightly. Refrigerate 6 hours or overnight; turn bag several times to distribute seasonings. Drain ribs; discard seasoning mixture. Place meat in deep roasting pan. Roast, uncovered, in 450° oven for 25 minutes. Drain off fat. Reduce oven temperature to 350°. Roast, covered, 30 minutes. Uncover; roast 30 minutes more. Makes 4 to 6 servings.

Pineapple Hawaiian Ribs

    3 pounds meaty pork spareribs, sawed in
        half across bones
    ¼ cup soy sauce
    ¼ cup dry sherry
    2 tablespoons finely chopped onion
    2 tablespoons molasses
    ½ teaspoon garlic powder
    ⅛ teaspoon pepper
    1 beaten egg
    ¼ cup cornstarch
    ¼ cup all-purpose flour
        Cooking oil for deep-fat frying
        Leaf lettuce *or* curly endive
        Pineapple-Orange Sauce

Cut meat into 2-rib portions. In Dutch oven simmer ribs, covered, in enough boiling water to cover for 30 minutes; drain. Place ribs in shallow baking dish.

To prepare marinade, combine soy sauce, dry sherry, onion, molasses, garlic powder, and pepper. Pour marinade over ribs; cover. Marinate for 1 hour at room temperature or 2 to 3 hours in the refrigerator, turning ribs occasionally. Drain; reserve marinade.

To make batter, combine reserved marinade, egg, cornstarch, and flour; beat till smooth. Dip ribs in batter. Fry spareribs, a few at a time, in deep hot oil (365°) for 1 to 2 minutes or till golden brown. Drain on paper toweling. Keep fried ribs warm in oven while cooking remaining ribs. Place ribs atop leaf lettuce or curly endive on platter; spoon some Pineapple-Orange Sauce over ribs. Pass remaining sauce. Serves 4 or 5.

Pineapple-Orange Sauce: Thoroughly rinse 1 *orange*. Cut peel from the orange. Using sharp knife remove white membrane and slice enough peel into julienne strips to measure 1 tablespoon. Section the orange over bowl to catch juice; add orange sections to juice and set aside. In covered saucepan simmer the orange peel strips in a small amount of water for 15 minutes; drain well.

Drain one 8¼-ounce can *pineapple chunks*, reserving ⅓ cup syrup. In a saucepan combine reserved pineapple syrup, ½ cup *water*, 2 tablespoons *vinegar*, 1 tablespoon *honey*, 1 teaspoon *instant chicken bouillon granules*, and ⅛ teaspoon *ground ginger*. Cook and stir till bubbly. Combine 1 tablespoon *cornstarch* and 1 tablespoon *cold water;* stir into vinegar mixture. Cook and stir till thickened and bubbly. Stir in orange sections and juice, drained orange peel, reserved pineapple chunks, and 2 teaspoons *orange liqueur*. Heat to boiling. Makes 2 cups.

Sweet and Pungent Ribs

3 pounds meaty pork spareribs, sawed in
  half across bones
¼ cup soy sauce
¼ cup dry sherry
1 tablespoon Five-Spice Powder
1 tablespoon vinegar
½ teaspoon salt
⅛ teaspoon pepper
1 beaten egg
¼ cup cornstarch
¼ cup all-purpose flour
  Cooking oil for deep-fat frying
  Sweet and Pungent Sauce

Cut meat into 2-rib portions. In Dutch oven simmer ribs, covered, in enough boiling water to
cover for 30 minutes; drain. Place ribs in a
12x7½x2-inch baking dish. For marinade combine soy sauce, sherry, Five-Spice Powder, vinegar, salt, and pepper; pour over ribs. Let stand
at room temperature for 30 minutes, turning
once. Drain spareribs, reserving marinade.

Combine reserved marinade, egg,
cornstarch, and flour; beat till smooth. Dip
spareribs in egg mixture. Fry ribs, a few at a
time, in deep hot oil (365°) for 1 to 2 minutes or
till golden brown. Drain on paper toweling. Keep
ribs warm in oven. Spoon some Sweet and Pungent Sauce over hot ribs to glaze. Serve with hot,
cooked *rice*. Pass remaining sauce. Makes 4 or
5 servings.

Five-Spice Powder: In small bowl combine 1
teaspoon ground *cinnamon*, 1 teaspoon
crushed *aniseed*, ¼ teaspoon crushed *fennel
seed*, ¼ teaspoon freshly ground *pepper or* ¼
teaspoon crushed *Szechwan pepper*, and ⅛
teaspoon ground *cloves*. (Or, purchase com-
mercial Five-Spice Powder at Oriental stores.)

Sweet and Pungent Sauce: Drain one 8¼-
ounce can *pineapple chunks*, reserving ⅓ cup
syrup. In saucepan combine the reserved syrup,
2 tablespoons *brown sugar*, 4 teaspoons
cornstarch, and ⅛ teaspoon *salt*. Stir in one
7½-ounce can *undrained tomatoes*, ¼ cup
finely chopped *onion*, 1 tablespoon *vinegar*, and
1 tablespoon *soy sauce*. Cook and stir till thickened and bubbly. Add pineapple chunks and 1
small *green pepper*, cut into 1-inch squares.
Heat through. Makes 2½ cups sauce.

Texas Barbecued Ribs

2 cups mesquite *or* hickory chips
4 pounds meaty pork spareribs
  Texas Barbecue Sauce (see recipe,
  page 88)

About an hour before cooking time, soak the
mesquite or hickory chips in enough water to
cover. In a covered grill place *hot* coals on both
sides of a foil drip pan. Drain chips. Sprinkle
coals with some chips. Place ribs atop grill over
drip pan. Brush with some of the Texas Barbecue Sauce. Lower grill hood. Grill 30 minutes,
adding additional coals and chips as needed.
Turn ribs, brushing both sides with sauce. Lower
grill hood; grill 30 minutes more, adding additional chips as needed. Brush ribs with sauce
during the last 20 minutes of cooking. Heat the
remaining sauce to pass with ribs. Serves 4 to 6.

Plantation Spareribs

½ cup molasses *or* sorghum
¼ cup prepared mustard
¼ cup vinegar
2 tablespoons worcestershire sauce
½ teaspoon salt
½ teaspoon bottled hot pepper sauce
4 pounds pork spareribs

Blend molasses or sorghum into mustard; stir in
remaining ingredients except ribs. Bring to boiling; set aside. Place ribs, meaty side down, in
shallow roasting pan. Roast, uncovered, in 450°
oven 30 minutes. Drain off fat. Turn ribs meaty
side up; season with salt. Reduce oven temperature to 350°; continue roasting for 1 hour or till
tender. During last 30 minutes of roasting, baste
frequently with sauce. Cut into serving-size
pieces. Makes 4 or 5 servings.

Microwave directions: Cut spareribs into
serving-size pieces. Season with salt. Arrange in
a 13x9x2-inch non-metal baking dish. Cover
with waxed paper. Cook in countertop microwave oven on high power for 12 minutes, giving
dish a half turn after 6 minutes. Drain; rearrange
ribs in dish and set aside. In 2-cup glass measure blend molasses or sorghum into mustard.
Stir in remaining ingredients. Micro-cook about 2
minutes or till mixture boils. Spoon over ribs.
Micro-cook, covered, 18 to 20 minutes or till
done. Rearrange ribs in dish and baste with molasses mixture every 5 minutes. Pass sauce.

Smoked Pineapple Ribs

Hickory chips
1 **teaspoon salt**
½ **teaspoon paprika**
½ **teaspoon ground turmeric**
6 **pounds pork loin back ribs** *or* **spareribs**
1 **8-ounce can crushed pineapple (juice pack)**
½ **cup packed brown sugar**
3 **tablespoons prepared mustard**
2 **tablespoons lemon juice**

About an hour before cooking time, soak hickory chips in enough water to cover. Combine salt, paprika, and turmeric; rub onto meaty side of ribs. Place ribs, meaty side up, over *slow* coals. Close hood or cover with foil tent; drain hickory chips. Cook ribs 30 minutes on each side sprinkling coals with dampened hickory chips every 20 minutes. (If thin end of spareribs cooks too quickly, place foil under end piece and continue cooking.) In saucepan combine *undrained* pineapple, brown sugar, mustard, and lemon juice. Heat and stir till sugar is dissolved. Brush some on ribs; cook 10 to 15 minutes more. Heat remainder and pass. Serves 6.

Teriyaki Appetizer Ribs

4 **pounds meaty pork spareribs, sawed in half across bones**
½ **cup soy sauce**
2 **tablespoons cooking oil**
2 **tablespoons lemon juice**
1 **tablespoon brown sugar**
2 **cloves garlic, minced**
1 **teaspoon ground ginger**
¼ **teaspoon pepper**
2 **tablespoons honey**

Cut meat into 2-rib portions. Mix remaining ingredients except honey. Place ribs in shallow pan; pour soy mixture over. Cover; marinate in refrigerator 4 to 6 hours or overnight. Occasionally spoon marinade over. Remove ribs, reserving marinade. Place ribs, meaty side up, over *slow* coals. Grill about 25 minutes (add less meaty ribs after about 10 minutes). Turn ribs, meaty side down; grill 15 to 20 minutes more. Stir honey into reserved marinade; brush often over ribs during last 5 minutes of grilling. Makes about 26 appetizers.

Spiced Apricot Ribs

1 **teaspoon salt**
1 **teaspoon ground ginger**
1 **teaspoon ground coriander**
½ **teaspoon paprika**
¼ **teaspoon pepper**
4 **pounds pork loin back ribs** *or* **spareribs**
Hickory chips
½ **cup apricot preserves**
¼ **cup orange juice**
3 **tablespoons soy sauce**
1 **tablespoon lemon juice**

Combine salt, ginger, coriander, paprika, and pepper; rub onto meaty side of ribs. Cover; refrigerate 2 hours. About an hour before cooking time, soak hickory chips in enough water to cover. Lace ribs on spit rod. Secure the ribs with holding fork. Arrange *hot* coals on both sides of a shallow foil drip pan. Drain hickory chips; sprinkle some over coals. Attach spit; position drip pan under meat. Turn on motor; lower the grill hood or cover with foil tent. Grill ribs over *hot* coals about 1 hour or till done. Sprinkle the coals with dampened hickory chips every 20 minutes. For glaze, combine remaining ingredients. Brush ribs frequently with glaze during the last 15 minutes of cooking. Heat and pass the remaining glaze. Makes 4 servings.

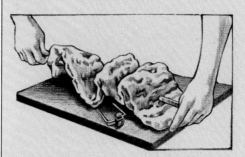

How to Barbecue Ribs

If your grill has a spit attachment, use it to barbecue long strips of pork spareribs or pork loin back ribs. Simply lace the ribs accordion-style on the spit. Secure the ribs using holding forks.

Ground Pork

Swiss-Style Meatballs

- 4 beaten eggs
- 2 cups light cream
- 6 slices white bread, toasted and torn up
- 1 medium onion, finely chopped (½ cup)
- 1 teaspoon salt
- ½ teaspoon ground nutmeg
- 2 pounds ground veal *or* ground beef
- 1 pound ground pork
- 3 tablespoons cooking oil
- 1 10¾-ounce can condensed cream of celery soup
- 2 tablespoons all-purpose flour

Combine eggs, *1 cup* of the cream, toasted bread, onion, salt, and nutmeg. Add meats; mix well. Shape into 36 1½-inch meatballs. In large skillet brown meatballs, a few at a time, in hot oil. Place in 13x9x2-inch baking dish. Discard excess drippings. In same skillet blend soup and the remaining 1 cup cream; pour over meatballs. Cover; bake in 325° oven about 1 hour. Place meatballs in serving dish; keep warm. Skim and discard excess fat from cream sauce; pour sauce into small saucepan. Blend ½ cup cold *water* into flour; stir into sauce. Cook and stir till thickened and bubbly. Pour over meatballs in dish. Makes 12 servings.

Shaping Meatballs

To shape meatballs to uniform size, form meat into a roll of desired diameter. Slice, as shown above; round into balls. (For 1-inch meatballs, use a 1-inch roll cut into 1-inch slices.) Or, pat meat to a square; cut into cubes, rounding each into a ball. (For 1-inch balls, use a 1-inch-thick square cut into 1-inch cubes.)

Sweet-Sour Meatballs

- 1 beaten egg
- ¼ cup milk
- ¾ cup soft bread crumbs
- ½ teaspoon ground ginger
- ¼ teaspoon pepper
- 1 pound ground pork
- ½ pound ground beef
- ½ cup raisins
- 2 tablespoons cooking oil
- 1¼ cups cranberry juice cocktail
- 1 8-ounce can whole cranberry sauce
- ½ cup bottled barbecue sauce
- ½ cup thin green pepper strips
- ½ cup cold water
- 1 tablespoon cornstarch
- ¼ cup sliced almonds, toasted

Combine egg, milk, bread crumbs, ginger, pepper, and ¾ teaspoon *salt*. Add meats and raisins; mix well. Shape into 36 one-inch meatballs. In 12-inch skillet brown meatballs in hot oil. Drain off fat. Combine cranberry juice cocktail, cranberry sauce, barbecue sauce, ¼ teaspoon *salt*, and dash *pepper*. Pour over meatballs. Bring to boiling. Cover; simmer 15 minutes. Add green pepper. Cover and simmer 5 minutes more. Blend cold water into cornstarch; add to skillet. Cook and stir till thickened and bubbly. Remove to serving platter. Sprinkle almonds atop. Serve with hot, cooked *rice*. Serves 6.

Glazed Pork-Bran Balls

- 1 beaten egg
- ⅓ cup milk
- 1 cup raisin bran flakes
- 1 tablespoon chopped onion
- ⅛ teaspoon salt
- ⅛ teaspoon dried thyme, crushed
- ½ pound ground pork
- ½ pound ground fully cooked ham
- ¼ cup packed brown sugar
- ¼ cup light corn syrup
- 1 tablespoon vinegar
- ½ teaspoon dry mustard

Combine egg, milk, bran flakes, onion, salt, thyme, and ⅛ teaspoon *pepper*. Add ground meats; mix well. Shape into 12 meatballs. Place in 11x7x1½-inch baking pan. Bake in 350° oven for 30 minutes. Spoon off fat. In small saucepan combine remaining ingredients; bring to boiling. Pour over meatballs. Bake about 20 minutes more, basting with sauce occasionally. Serves 4.

Cranberry juice cocktail, barbecue sauce, and ginger spark up the flavor of Sweet-Sour Meatballs.

Pork Burgers

1   pound ground pork
2   tablespoons chopped green onion
¾ teaspoon salt
¼ teaspoon ground sage
⅛ teaspoon pepper
4   hamburger buns, split and toasted

Combine all ingredients except buns. Shape into 4 patties, ½ inch thick. Place patties on unheated rack in broiler pan. Broil patties 3 inches from heat for 8 minutes. Turn; broil 7 minutes more. (Or, pan-broil patties. Preheat heavy skillet. Cook patties over medium heat for 6 to 7 minutes per side, or till done. Partially cover skillet to prevent spattering.) Serve on toasted hamburger buns. Serves 4.

Egg Rolls

¾ pound ground pork
1   clove garlic, minced
1   tablespoon cooking oil
2   cups finely chopped bok choy
1   cup finely chopped fresh mushrooms
½ cup thinly sliced green onion
½ cup finely chopped water chestnuts
½ cup finely shredded carrot
2   tablespoons soy sauce
2   teaspoons cornstarch
½ teaspoon sugar
12 Chinese egg roll skins
     Cooking oil for deep-fat frying
     Sweet and Sour Sauce

In skillet stir-fry pork and garlic in 1 tablespoon hot oil till meat is browned. Drain off fat. Add vegetables; stir-fry 2 to 3 minutes more. Blend soy into cornstarch; stir in sugar and ¼ teaspoon *salt*. Stir into pork mixture; cook and stir till thickened. Cool. Wrap egg rolls using directions at right. Fry egg rolls, a few at a time, in deep hot fat (365°) for 2 to 3 minutes or till golden brown. Remove; drain on paper toweling. Serve warm with Sweet and Sour Sauce. Makes 12 egg rolls.

Sweet and Sour Sauce: In a small saucepan combine ½ cup packed *brown sugar* and 1 tablespoon *cornstarch*. Stir in ⅓ cup *red wine vinegar*, ⅓ cup *water*, ¼ cup finely chopped *green pepper*, 2 tablespoons chopped *pimiento*, 1 tablespoon *soy sauce*, ¼ teaspoon *instant chicken bouillon granules*, ¼ teaspoon *garlic powder*, and ¼ teaspoon *ground ginger*. Cook and stir till bubbly. Serve warm. Makes 1¼ cups sauce.

Hearty Sauced Burgers

1   beaten egg
2   tablespoons water
2   tablespoons catsup
¼ cup fine dry bread crumbs
½ teaspoon salt
¼ teaspoon onion salt
¼ teaspoon dried oregano, crushed
2   pounds ground pork
8   hamburger buns, split and toasted
     Pepper-Onion Sauce

Combine first 7 ingredients. Add meat; mix well. Shape into 8 patties, ½ inch thick. Place patties on unheated rack in broiler pan. Broil patties 3 inches from heat for 8 minutes. Turn; broil 7 minutes more. Serve on hamburger buns. Top meat with Pepper-Onion Sauce. Serves 8.

Pepper-Onion Sauce: Cook ⅓ cup finely chopped *onion* and ⅓ cup finely chopped *green pepper* in 3 tablespoons *butter* till onion is tender but not brown. Add ¾ cup *catsup*, 2 tablespoons *brown sugar*, 1 teaspoon *prepared horseradish*, and ½ teaspoon *salt;* heat through. Makes 1 cup.

Wrapping Egg Rolls

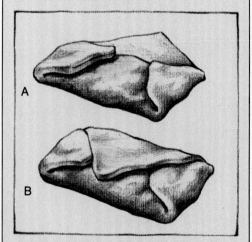

(A) Place egg roll skin so one point is toward you. Spoon about ¼ cup filling horizontally across and just below center of skin. Fold bottom point of skin over filling; tuck point under filling. Fold sides in. (B) Roll up toward remaining corner; moisten point and press firmly to seal.

Pork Strata

- 1 **pound ground pork**
- ½ **cup chopped onion**
- ¼ **cup chopped green pepper**
- 1 **2-ounce can chopped mushrooms**
- 5 **cups dry bread cubes (7 slices)**
- 4 **beaten eggs**
- 1 **10¾-ounce can condensed cream of mushroom soup**
- 1¼ **cups milk**
- ½ **cup mayonnaise *or* salad dressing**
- ¾ **teaspoon dried thyme, crushed**
  Dash cayenne
- 2 **tablespoons butter *or* margarine**

Cook pork, onion, and green pepper till meat is browned; drain off fat. Drain mushrooms; stir into meat with ¼ teaspoon *salt.* Place *2 cups* of the bread cubes in a 12x7½x2-inch baking dish. Sprinkle meat mixture over bread in dish. Top with another *2 cups* bread cubes. Combine eggs, soup, milk, mayonnaise, thyme, and cayenne. Pour over ingredients in baking dish. Cover; chill at least 1 hour. Toss remaining bread cubes with butter; sprinkle atop. Bake, uncovered, in a 325° oven about 50 minutes. Let stand 10 minutes before serving. Serves 8.

Pork Loaf Supreme

- 1 **beaten egg**
- 1 **cup dairy sour cream**
- 1 **cup finely shredded carrot**
- 1 **cup finely crushed saltine crackers**
- ¼ **cup chopped onion**
- 1 **teaspoon prepared mustard**
- 1 **pound ground pork**
- 1 **pound ground beef**
  Sour Cream Sauce

Combine first 6 ingredients, ¾ teaspoon *salt,* and ¼ teaspoon *pepper.* Add meats; mix well. Press into 9x5x3-inch loaf pan. Bake in 350° oven about 1½ hours. Drain off fat. Let stand in pan 10 minutes. Serve with Sour Cream Sauce. Serves 8.

Sour Cream Sauce: Dissolve ½ teaspoon *instant beef bouillon granules* in ½ cup boiling *water;* cool. In saucepan melt 2 tablespoons *butter;* stir in one 2-ounce can *chopped mushrooms,* drained, and dash *pepper.* In bowl combine ¼ cup *dairy sour cream* and 1 tablespoon *all-purpose flour;* slowly stir in cooled bouillon. Add sour cream mixture to mushrooms in saucepan. Cook till heated; *do not boil.*

Pork and Apple Pie

- 1 **pound ground pork**
- 1 **medium onion, finely chopped (½ cup)**
- ½ **cup fine dry bread crumbs**
- ½ **cup chicken broth**
  Pastry for Double-Crust Pie (see recipe, page 42)
- 2 **medium cooking apples, peeled, cored and sliced (2 cups)**
- 2 **tablespoons brown sugar**
- ¼ **teaspoon ground cinnamon**

In skillet cook pork and onion till pork is browned. Remove from heat. Stir in bread crumbs, broth, 1 teaspoon *salt,* and dash *pepper.* Line a 9-inch pie plate with *half* the pastry; fill with meat mixture. Combine apples, brown sugar, and cinnamon; spoon atop meat layer. Adjust top crust; seal and flute edges. Cut slits in top crust. Bake in 400° oven for 35 to 40 minutes or till golden brown. Let stand 10 minutes before serving. Makes 6 servings.

Pork and Liver Pâté

- 2 **slices bacon, halved**
- ½ **cup chopped onion**
- 2 **cloves garlic, minced**
- 1 **pound ground pork**
- ¼ **pound chicken livers**
- 1 **cup milk**
- 2 **eggs**
- 2 **tablespoons fine dry bread crumbs**
- 2 **tablespoons anchovy paste**
- 1 **tablespoon cornstarch**
- 2 **teaspoons prepared mustard**
- ½ **teaspoon dried sage, crushed**
- ½ **teaspoon dried basil, crushed**

Cook bacon till crisp. Set bacon aside; reserve 2 tablespoons drippings. In drippings cook onion and garlic till onion is tender. Add ground pork and chicken livers. Cook and stir over medium-high heat about 5 minutes or till livers are no longer pink. Drain well; cool. In blender container place ½ *cup* of the milk, the pork-onion mixture, and bacon. Cover; blend on medium speed till smooth. Add remaining ingredients, ¼ teaspoon *salt,* and ⅛ teaspoon *pepper.* Cover; blend thoroughly. Pour into an 8x4x2-inch loaf pan. Set in shallow baking pan; pour hot water around loaf pan to depth of ½ inch. Bake in 325° oven for 1 hour. Cool; cover and chill. To serve, unmold and slice; spread on crisp crackers. Makes about 4 cups.

Boneless Pork

Pork-Brown Rice Skillet

- 1 **pound boneless pork, cut into 1-inch cubes**
- ½ **cup chopped onion**
- 2 **tablespoons cooking oil**
- 2¼ **cups water**
- 1 **cup brown rice**
- 2 **teaspoons instant chicken bouillon granules**
- 2 **medium apples, peeled, cored, and chopped**
- ½ **cup sliced celery**
- ½ **cup raisins**
- ¼ **cup sliced blanched almonds**

In skillet cook pork and onion in hot oil till onion is tender but not brown. Stir in water, uncooked rice, bouillon granules, ½ teaspoon *salt,* and dash *pepper.* Bring to boiling. Cover; simmer about 25 minutes. Stir in apple, celery, and raisins. Cover; simmer for 20 to 25 minutes more or till rice and celery are tender. To serve, sprinkle almonds atop. Makes 6 servings.

Pork and Brew

- 2 **pounds boneless pork, cut into 1-inch cubes**
- 3 **tablespoons cooking oil**
- 1 **12-ounce can beer**
- ½ **cup water**
- 1 **tablespoon brown sugar**
- 2 **teaspoons instant beef bouillon granules**
- 1 **clove garlic, minced**
- 1 **bay leaf**
- ½ **teaspoon dried thyme, crushed**
- 3 **medium onions, sliced (1½ cups)**
  Beef stock
- 3 **tablespoons all-purpose flour**

In large skillet brown the meat, half at a time, in hot oil. Return all meat to skillet. Reserve ¼ cup beer; combine remaining beer, next 6 ingredients, and ¼ teaspoon *pepper.* Pour over meat. Add onions. Cover; simmer about 50 minutes or till meat is tender. Remove meat and onions to serving bowl; keep warm. Skim excess fat from juices; remove bay leaf. Measure pan juices. Add enough beef stock to juices to measure 1½ cups. Blend reserved beer into flour; stir into pan juices. Cook and stir till thickened and bubbly. Season with salt and pepper. Pour gravy over meat and serve with hot, cooked *noodles.* Makes 6 to 8 servings.

German Pork and Kraut

- 4 **slices bacon**
- 2 **pounds boneless pork, cut into 1-inch cubes**
- 1 **cup chopped onion**
- 2 **cloves garlic, minced**
- 1 **27-ounce can *or* two 16-ounce cans sauerkraut, drained**
- 1 **cup dry white wine**
- ½ **cup water**
- 6 **whole black peppercorns**
- 6 **juniper berries (optional)**
- 1 **bay leaf**
- ½ **teaspoon instant chicken bouillon granules**
- ½ **teaspoon dried thyme, crushed**

In large skillet cook bacon till crisp; drain, reserving 2 tablespoons drippings. Crumble bacon; set aside. In same skillet cook meat, onion, and garlic in drippings till meat is browned and onion is tender. Remove from heat. Stir in bacon, remaining ingredients, and 1 teaspoon *salt.* Turn into a 3-quart casserole. Bake, covered, in 325° oven for 1¾ to 2 hours or till pork is tender. Remove peppercorns, juniper berries, and bay leaf. Makes 6 servings.

Cubing Tip

If you check prices, you may find it is more economical to cut your own pork cubes from lean boneless pork. Some larger cuts to choose from are boneless shoulder roasts, boneless loin roasts, or loin blade roasts.

To cut a roast into 1-inch cubes, first trim excess fat from roast. Cut roast into 1-inch slices, then cut into 1-inch pieces.

Marinated Pork Kabobs

- 1 cup dry white wine
- ½ cup cooking oil
- 2 teaspoons paprika
- 1 clove garlic, minced
- 1 bay leaf
- ½ teaspoon salt
- ¼ teaspoon pepper
- 1½ pounds boneless pork, cut into 1-inch cubes
- 1 pound boiling onions (16)
- 4 large carrots, cut into 1-inch pieces

Mix first 7 ingredients. Place meat in plastic bag; pour wine mixture over meat. Close bag and set in deep bowl. Refrigerate 6 to 8 hours or overnight, turning bag occasionally. Drain pork, reserving marinade; discard bay leaf. Cook onions and carrots in small amount of boiling salted water for about 15 to 20 minutes or till nearly tender; drain. On six skewers alternately thread pork cubes, onions, and carrots. Broil 4 inches from heat for about 25 minutes, turning once. Brush with marinade occasionally and just before serving. Makes 6 servings.

Dilled Pork Bundles

- 1 large onion, chopped (1 cup)
- ¾ cup chopped fresh mushrooms
- 2 tablespoons butter or margarine
- ¾ pound boneless pork, coarsely chopped
- ½ cup dairy sour cream
- 1 teaspoon lemon juice
- ½ teaspoon salt
- ½ teaspoon dried dillweed
- 2 packages (16 rolls) refrigerated crescent rolls

Cook onion and mushrooms in butter or margarine till tender but not brown; push to one side of skillet. Add pork; cook and stir over medium-high heat 5 to 6 minutes or till pork is browned. Reduce heat; stir in sour cream, lemon juice, salt, and dillweed. Heat through; *do not boil*. Unroll crescent roll dough; form into eight 6x3½-inch rectangles by pressing perforated edges together. Spoon about ¼ cup pork filling onto half of each dough rectangle. Fold over other half of dough; seal edges with tines of fork. Place on ungreased baking sheet. If desired, brush tops with milk. Bake in a 425° oven about 10 minutes or till golden brown. Makes 8 sandwiches.

Double Nut Pork Kabobs

- ¾ cup coarsely chopped fresh coconut
- ½ cup creamy peanut butter
- ¼ cup coarsely chopped onion
- 3 tablespoons soy sauce
- 2 teaspoons lime juice
- ½ teaspoon ground coriander
- ½ teaspoon ground ginger
- 3 drops bottled hot pepper sauce
- 2 pounds boneless pork, cut into 1-inch cubes

Place all ingredients except pork in blender container; cover and blend till smooth, scraping down sides of blender as needed. Coat pork cubes with nut mixture. Refrigerate for 2 to 3 hours or overnight. Thread meat on skewers. Broil 3 to 4 inches from heat for 20 to 25 minutes or till coating is crusty and pork is done. Turn skewers occasionally. Serve with hot, cooked *rice*. Makes 6 to 8 servings.

Sweet-Sour Pork

- 1 beaten egg
- ¼ cup cornstarch
- ¼ cup all-purpose flour
- 1½ cups chicken broth
- 1 pound boneless pork, cut into 1-inch cubes
  Cooking oil for deep-fat frying
- 1 large green pepper, chopped
- ½ cup chopped carrot
- 1 clove garlic, minced
- 2 tablespoons cooking oil
- ½ cup sugar
- ⅓ cup red wine vinegar
- 2 teaspoons soy sauce
- 2 tablespoons cornstarch

In a bowl combine egg, the ¼ cup cornstarch, flour, ¼ *cup* of the chicken broth, and ½ teaspoon *salt;* beat till smooth. Dip pork cubes in batter. Fry in deep hot oil (365°) for 5 to 6 minutes or till golden. Drain; keep warm. In skillet cook green pepper, carrot, and garlic in the 2 tablespoons oil till vegetables are tender but not brown. Stir in remaining 1¼ cups chicken broth, sugar, vinegar, and soy sauce. Bring to boiling; boil rapidly 1 minute. Blend ¼ cup cold *water* into the 2 tablespoons cornstarch. Stir into vegetable mixture. Cook and stir till thickened and bubbly. Stir in pork cubes. Serve with hot, cooked *rice,* if desired. Makes 4 to 6 servings.

Wine and herbs make Pork-Noodle Stew special, and zucchini and tomato team in Pork Oven-Style Burgoo.

Pork-Noodle Stew

    2 slices bacon
 1½ pounds boneless pork, cut into
        ½-inch cubes
    1 cup chopped onion
    1 clove garlic, minced
    3 10½-ounce cans condensed beef broth
    5 cups water
    1 cup dry white wine
    1 bay leaf
    1 teaspoon dried marjoram, crushed
  ½ teaspoon salt
  ¼ to ½ teaspoon pepper
    3 ounces medium noodles
    2 medium carrots, bias sliced (1 cup)
    1 4-ounce can sliced mushrooms, drained
    1 10-ounce package frozen peas
    3 tablespoons cornstarch
        Snipped fresh chives

In Dutch oven cook bacon till crisp; remove bacon, crumble, and set aside. Reserve drippings. Brown the pork, onion, and garlic, half at a time, in drippings. Return all meat and onion to Dutch oven; drain off fat. Add condensed beef broth, water, wine, bay leaf, marjoram, salt, and pepper. Cover; simmer for 1 hour. Stir in *uncooked* noodles, carrots, and mushrooms. Bring mixture to full boil; cover and simmer 5 minutes. Add frozen peas; simmer 5 minutes more or till noodles and vegetables are tender. Remove bay leaf. Blend cornstarch and 3 tablespoons *cold water;* add to stew. Cook and stir till slightly thickened and bubbly. Ladle into soup bowls. Sprinkle crumbled bacon and fresh chives over each serving. Serves 6.

Pork and Fruit Kabobs

    1 8¼-ounce can pineapple slices
  ⅓ cup orange marmalade
    2 tablespoons soy sauce
 1½ pounds boneless pork, cut into 1-inch
        cubes
    2 medium cooking apples, cored and cut
        into 6 wedges each

Drain pineapple; reserve 2 tablespoons syrup. Quarter each slice; set aside. In saucepan combine reserved syrup, marmalade, and soy. Heat till marmalade melts. Thread six skewers alternately with pork, pineapple, and apples. Grill over *medium* coals about 15 minutes, turning and brushing often with marmalade mixture. Serves 6.

Pork Oven-Style Burgoo

    2 pounds boneless pork
    2 tablespoons cooking oil
    1 clove garlic, minced
    1 18-ounce can (2¼ cups) tomato juice
  ½ cup dry white wine
  ½ cup cold water
  ¼ cup all-purpose flour
    2 teaspoons instant chicken bouillon
        granules
    1 teaspoon sugar
    1 teaspoon dried oregano, crushed
    4 medium carrots, bias sliced into ¼-inch
        slices (2 cups)
 1½ cups whole pearl onions *or* frozen small
        whole onions
  ½ cup chopped green pepper
    1 16-ounce can tomatoes, cut up
    1 medium zucchini (6 ounces), sliced

Partially freeze meat. Slice pork thinly across the grain into bite-size strips, about 2x½-inches. In large skillet brown half the pork in hot oil; remove and set aside. Brown remaining pork and garlic. Remove all meat to a 3-quart casserole, leaving any meat juices in skillet. Add tomato juice and wine to skillet. Blend water into flour. Add flour mixture, bouillon granules, sugar, oregano, and 1 teaspoon *salt* to mixture in skillet. Cook and stir till thickened and bubbly. Pour over meat in casserole. Bake, covered, in 350° oven about 40 minutes. Stir in carrots, onions, and green pepper. Bake, covered, for 30 minutes more. Add *undrained* tomatoes and zucchini; bake, uncovered, 15 to 20 minutes, stirring occasionally, till meat and vegetables are tender. Stir before serving. Makes 8 servings.

Zesty Pork Chili

    1 pound boneless pork, cut into ¾-inch
        cubes
    2 tablespoons cooking oil
    4 to 6 teaspoons chili powder
  ½ teaspoon salt
    1 clove garlic, minced
    2 medium potatoes, peeled and cut into
        1-inch cubes (2 cups)

In large saucepan brown the meat, half at a time, in hot oil. Drain off fat; return all meat to pan. Stir in chili powder, salt, garlic, and 1 cup *water.* Cover; simmer 35 minutes. Stir in potatoes. Cover; simmer 20 to 25 minutes more or till meat and potatoes are tender. Serves 4.

Pork in Pineapple Sauce

The right amount of vinegar blends with just the right amount of brown sugar to make sweet-sour sauce that coats pork, pineapple, and green pepper –

1½ **pounds boneless pork, cut into ½-inch cubes**
  2 **tablespoons cooking oil**
  ¼ **cup chopped onion**
  ¼ **cup water**
  1 **15¼-ounce can pineapple chunks (juice pack)**
  ¼ **cup packed brown sugar**
  2 **tablespoons cornstarch**
  ¼ **teaspoon salt**
  ¼ **teaspoon ground ginger**
  ¼ **cup vinegar**
  3 **tablespoons soy sauce**
  1 **medium green pepper, cut into 1-inch squares**

In large skillet brown the pork cubes, half at a time, in hot cooking oil. Return all the browned meat to the skillet. Add the chopped onion and water. Cover and simmer the meat and onion for 30 to 35 minutes.

Drain pineapple chunks, reserving the juice. Set pineapple chunks aside. In a bowl combine the brown sugar, cornstarch, salt, and ground ginger. Blend in the reserved pineapple juice, vinegar, and soy sauce till thoroughly combined. Add to pork mixture in skillet along with the green pepper squares. Cook and stir till mixture is thickened and bubbly. Stir in the drained pineapple chunks and heat through. Serve mixture over hot, cooked *rice.* Makes 6 servings.

Microwave directions: In a 2-quart, non-metal casserole combine the brown sugar, cornstarch, salt, and ginger. Stir in the water, vinegar, and soy sauce. Add pork cubes, *undrained* pineapple, and chopped onion. Stir to coat pork. Cover casserole with lid, waxed paper, or clear plastic wrap. Cook in countertop microwave oven on high power for 14 minutes, stirring once after 7 minutes. Stir in the green pepper squares. Cover casserole, and micro-cook 1 minute more. Serve mixture over hot, cooked *rice.*

Pork and Vegetable Stew

1½ **pounds boneless pork, cut into ¾-inch cubes**
  2 **tablespoons cooking oil**
  1 **10½-ounce can condensed beef broth**
  1 **bay leaf**
  1 **teaspoon prepared mustard**
  ½ **teaspoon dried thyme, crushed**
  3 **medium carrots, cut into 1-inch pieces**
  3 **medium potatoes, peeled and quartered**
  1 **10-ounce package frozen whole kernel corn**
  1 **cup pearl onions**
  2 **tablespoons all-purpose flour**

In Dutch oven brown meat, half at a time, in hot oil. Return all meat to pan. Stir in next 4 ingredients, ½ cup *water,* 1 teaspoon *salt,* and ¼ teaspoon *pepper.* Bring to boiling. Cover; simmer 30 minutes or till meat is almost tender. Add carrots and potatoes. Cover; simmer 15 minutes. Add corn and onions. Cover; simmer 10 minutes or till vegetables are tender. Blend ¼ cup cold *water* into flour; stir into stew. Cook and stir till bubbly. Remove bay leaf. Serves 6.

Pork Chop Suey

  1 **pound boneless pork, cut into ¾-inch cubes**
  1 **clove garlic, minced**
  1 **tablespoon cooking oil**
  ¼ **cup soy sauce**
  2 **teaspoons instant chicken bouillon granules**
1½ **cups bias-sliced celery**
  1 **medium onion, cut into wedges**
  1 **16-ounce can bean sprouts, drained**
  1 **8-ounce can water chestnuts, drained and thinly sliced**
  1 **6-ounce package frozen pea pods, thawed and halved crosswise**
  ½ **cup thinly sliced fresh mushrooms**
  2 **tablespoons cornstarch**

In large skillet brown pork and garlic in hot oil. Add soy, bouillon granules, and 1½ cups *water.* Cover; simmer for 30 minutes. Add celery and onion. Cook 5 minutes; stir occasionally. Add next 4 ingredients. Blend 2 tablespoons *cold water* into cornstarch; stir into meat. Cook and stir till vegetables are crisp-tender and mixture is thickened and bubbly. Serve with hot, cooked *rice.* Pass additional soy sauce. Serves 4 to 6.

Pork-Wonton Soup

Buy wonton skins at a supermarket or Oriental food store. If wonton skins are not available, purchase egg roll skins and cut each into quarters –

1½ pounds boneless pork, cut into
      ½-inch cubes
½ cup chopped onion
1 clove garlic, minced
2 tablespoons cooking oil
6 cups water
½ cup dry white wine
2 tablespoons soy sauce
4 teaspoons instant chicken bouillon
      granules
2 teaspoons sugar
½ teaspoon ground ginger
1 beaten egg yolk
⅔ cup finely chopped bok choy
2 tablespoons finely chopped onion
¼ teaspoon sugar
     Dash ground ginger
20 wonton skins
2 cups coarsely chopped bok choy
1 cup sliced fresh mushrooms
1 6-ounce package frozen pea pods

In 4½-quart Dutch oven cook half the meat, ½ cup chopped onion, and garlic in hot oil till meat is browned. Remove from pan. Brown remaining meat in oil. Drain. Return all to Dutch oven. Add water, wine, soy sauce, bouillon granules, 2 teaspoons sugar, and ½ teaspoon ground ginger to Dutch oven. Bring to boiling; reduce heat. Cover and simmer about 1½ hours or till meat is tender, stirring occasionally.

Meanwhile, prepare wontons. In bowl combine egg yolk, ⅔ cup finely chopped bok choy, 2 tablespoons finely chopped onion, ¼ teaspoon sugar, and dash ground ginger. Fill and wrap wontons with bok choy mixture, using directions in tip box at right. Use about 1 teaspoon of the filling per wonton skin.

In large saucepan cook wontons in a large amount of boiling water for 3 to 5 minutes. Drain and keep warm.

Add the 2 cups bok choy, the mushrooms, and pea pods to the pork mixture. Simmer about 3 minutes more. Add warm wontons. Makes 6 servings.

Pork and Cabbage Soup

1 pound boneless pork, cut into
      ½-inch cubes
1 tablespoon cooking oil
1 10¾-ounce can condensed tomato soup
1 10½-ounce can condensed beef broth
¼ cup dry sherry
1 small head cabbage, shredded (4 cups)
½ cup chopped onion
1 bay leaf
½ teaspoon paprika
     Dairy sour cream
     Snipped parsley

In 4½-quart Dutch oven brown pork in hot oil. Drain off excess fat. Blend in next 3 ingredients and 2½ cups *water.* Stir in next 4 ingredients, 1 teaspoon *salt,* and dash *pepper.* Bring to boiling. Reduce heat; cover and simmer about 40 minutes or till meat is tender. Season to taste. Remove bay leaf. Top servings with sour cream; sprinkle with parsley. Serves 5 or 6.

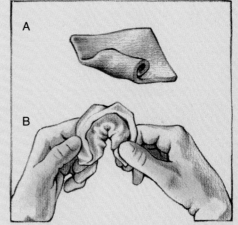

Wrapping Wontons

A

B

Position wonton skin with one point toward you. Spoon filling just below center. (A) Fold bottom point of wonton skin over filling and roll up, leaving about 1 inch unrolled at top. Moisten right-hand corner of skin with water. (B) Grasp right and left corners. Bring these corners toward you below filling. Overlap left corner over right corner. Press to seal.

Pork with Fresh Pineapple

Partially freezing the meat makes it easier to slice into bite-size strips. Use either a wok or a large skillet to prepare this stir-fried main dish –

- 1 **pound boneless pork (see Note)**
- 1 **small pineapple**
- ¼ **cup soy sauce**
- 1 **tablespoon cornstarch**
- ½ **teaspoon finely shredded orange peel**
- ½ **cup orange juice**
- ¼ **cup dry sherry**
- ½ **teaspoon instant chicken bouillon granules**
- 2 **tablespoons cooking oil**
- 1 **clove garlic, minced**
- 2 **medium green peppers, cut into ¾-inch pieces**
- 1 **8-ounce can water chestnuts, drained and sliced**

Partially freeze pork; slice thinly into bite-size strips. Set meat aside.

Twist the crown off the pineapple and cut off the base. Slice off strips of rind lengthwise, then remove eyes of fruit by cutting narrow wedge-shaped grooves in the pineapple. Cut off the hard center core of pineapple as you slice the fruit. Cut into chunks, reserving any juice.

In small bowl blend soy sauce into cornstarch; stir in reserved pineapple juice, orange peel, orange juice, dry sherry, and chicken bouillon granules. Set mixture aside.

Preheat a wok or large skillet over high heat; add cooking oil. Stir-fry garlic in hot oil 30 seconds. Add green pepper pieces; stir-fry 1 minute. Add water chestnuts; stir-fry 1 minute more. Remove green peppers and water chestnuts. (Add more oil, if necessary.)

Add the pork to *hot* wok or skillet; stir-fry 3 to 4 minutes. Stir soy sauce mixture and stir into pork. Cook and stir till thickened and bubbly. Stir in the pineapple chunks, green peppers, and water chestnuts; cover and heat 2 to 3 minutes. Serve at once with hot, cooked *rice*. Makes 4 servings.

Note: For the 1 pound boneless pork, a good choice would be pork tenderloin.

Pork-Vegetable Stir-Fry

- 1 **pound boneless pork**
- ½ **teaspoon instant chicken bouillon granules**
- 3 **tablespoons soy sauce**
- 2 **teaspoons cornstarch**
- 2 **tablespoons cooking oil**
- 1 **teaspoon grated gingerroot**
- 6 **cups small fresh spinach leaves**
- 1 **cup bias-sliced celery**
- 10 **green onions, bias sliced into 1-inch lengths (1 cup)**
- 2 **cups thinly sliced fresh mushrooms**
- 2 **cups fresh bean sprouts *or* one 16-ounce can bean sprouts, drained**
- 1 **8-ounce can water chestnuts, drained and thinly sliced**

Partially freeze pork; slice thinly into bite-size pieces. Dissolve bouillon granules in ⅓ cup boiling *water*. Blend soy into cornstarch; stir in bouillon. Preheat wok or large skillet over high heat; add cooking oil. Stir-fry gingerroot in hot oil 30 seconds. Add spinach, celery, and onions to wok; stir-fry 2 minutes. Remove vegetables. (Add more oil, if needed.) Add mushrooms, bean sprouts, and water chestnuts to wok. Stir-fry 1 minute. Remove vegetables. Add pork to hot wok; stir-fry 2 minutes. Stir soy mixture; stir into pork. Cook and stir till bubbly. Add all vegetables. Cover; cook 1 minute. Makes 6 servings.

Side Pork Fry

- 1 **pound fresh side pork, sliced**
- ¼ **cup yellow cornmeal**
- 2 **tablespoons all-purpose flour**
- ½ **teaspoon salt**
- ⅛ **teaspoon pepper**
- ⅛ **teaspoon paprika**
   Fried Apples

Remove the rind from side pork, if desired. Combine cornmeal, flour, salt, pepper, and paprika; coat pork slices with mixture. In skillet cook pork slices on both sides over medium heat for 18 to 20 minutes or till crisp. Serve with Fried Apples. Makes 4 servings.

Fried Apples: Core 4 tart *apples;* thinly slice into rings. In skillet melt ¼ cup *butter or margarine.* Add apple rings and ¼ cup packed *brown sugar.* Cover and cook about 10 minutes or till apples are tender and translucent, stirring occasionally. Sprinkle apple slices with ground *cinnamon, nutmeg, or cardamom.*

Fresh vegetables, sliced pork, and Oriental seasonings quickly cook in a wok or skillet for Pork-Vegetable Stir-Fry.

Cooked Pork

Individual Pork Pot Pies

½ cup chopped celery
½ cup chopped onion
¼ cup snipped parsley
3 tablespoons butter *or* margarine
½ cup all-purpose flour
1 tablespoon instant chicken bouillon
   granules
¼ teaspoon ground sage
¼ teaspoon dried thyme, crushed
¼ teaspoon salt
⅛ teaspoon pepper
2 cups water
1 cup milk
2½ cups chopped cooked pork
1 10-ounce package frozen peas
1 2-ounce jar sliced pimiento, drained
   and chopped
   Pastry for Double-Crust Pie
   Milk

In large saucepan cook celery, onion, and parsley in butter or margarine till vegetables are tender. Blend in flour, bouillon granules, sage, thyme, salt, and pepper. Stir in water and the 1 cup milk all at once; cook and stir till mixture is thickened and bubbly. Stir in pork, peas, and pimiento. Divide mixture into eight 4¼x1-inch round pie plates (about ¾ cup each).

Prepare Pastry; divide in half. On floured surface roll each half into a 12-inch square. Cut four 6-inch circles out of each half of pastry. Place one circle atop each pie; seal to edge of plate. Cut slits in top for escape of steam. Brush with a little milk. Bake, uncovered, in 425° oven for 25 to 30 minutes or till golden. Cover edges with foil last few minutes of baking, if needed, to prevent overbrowning. Serves 8.

Pastry for Double-Crust Pie: In medium mixing bowl stir together 2 cups all-purpose *flour* and 1 teaspoon *salt*. Cut in ⅔ cup *shortening or lard* till pieces are the size of small peas. Using 6 to 7 tablespoons *cold water*, sprinkle 1 tablespoon water over part of mixture; gently toss with a fork. Push to side of bowl. Repeat till all is moistened. Form dough into 2 balls.

Note: To freeze pot pies, prepare as above except do not cut slits in pastry or brush with milk. Freeze unbaked pies just till firm. Wrap, label, and place in freezer.

Thaw frozen pies 10 minutes while oven preheats. Cut slits in top crust and brush with milk. Bake frozen pies in 425° oven for 40 to 45 minutes. Or, thaw in refrigerator 5 hours. Cut slits in top crust and brush with milk. Bake in 425° oven for 30 to 35 minutes.

Chinese Fried Rice with Pork

2 beaten eggs
1 tablespoon cooking oil
¼ cup sliced green onion
1 clove garlic, minced
1 tablespoon cooking oil
4 cups cooked rice
½ cup coarsely shredded cooked pork
3 tablespoons soy sauce
¼ teaspoon crushed red pepper
   Soy sauce

In 12-inch skillet cook eggs in 1 tablespoon cooking oil, without stirring, till set. Invert skillet over a baking sheet to remove cooked eggs; cut into short, narrow strips. In the same skillet cook green onion and garlic in 1 tablespoon cooking oil till onion is tender. Stir in cooked rice, shredded cooked pork, the 3 tablespoons soy sauce, the red pepper, and egg strips. Heat through. If desired, sprinkle with additional sliced green onion. Pass soy sauce. Makes 6 to 8 servings.

Quick Pork-Potato Chowder

1 4⅝- *or* 5½-ounce package dry scalloped
   potato mix
3 cups water
1 10-ounce package frozen peas and
   carrots
4 cups milk
2 cups cubed cooked pork
1 teaspoon minced dried onion
1½ cups shredded American cheese
   (6 ounces)

In a Dutch oven or large saucepan combine the potatoes from the scalloped potato mix with the water. Bring to boiling. Reduce heat; cover and simmer for 5 minutes. Add frozen peas and carrots. Return to boiling. Reduce heat; cover and simmer for 10 minutes or till potatoes are tender, stirring occasionally. Stir in milk, pork, onion, and the seasoning packet from the scalloped potato mix. Cook and stir till bubbly. Stir in cheese; cook and stir till cheese melts. Makes 6 to 8 servings.

Beans Azteca

    1 medium onion, chopped (½ cup)
    ½ cup chopped green pepper
    2 15-ounce cans red kidney beans,
        drained
    2 cups chopped cooked pork
    1 12-ounce can whole kernel corn,
        drained
 1½ cups tortilla chips, crushed
    ¾ cup bottled barbecue sauce
    2 to 3 teaspoons chili powder
    1 8-ounce jar cheese spread
        Pickled whole peppers (optional)

In saucepan cook onion and green pepper in a small amount of boiling water about 5 minutes or till tender. Drain. Combine cooked vegetable mixture, beans, pork, corn, tortilla chips, barbecue sauce, and chili powder. Turn one-third of meat mixture into an ungreased 2½-quart casserole; spread ½ cup cheese spread over meat. Repeat layers; top with remaining meat mixture. Cover and refrigerate up to 24 hours. Bake, covered, in a 375° oven for 1¼ hours or till heated through. Garnish with pickled whole peppers, if desired. Makes 6 servings.

Vegetable-Noodle Soup

 2½ cups water
    1 17-ounce can cream-style corn
    1 16-ounce can tomatoes, cut up
    1 10½-ounce can condensed beef broth
    2 small zucchini, thinly sliced
        (about 2 cups)
    1 medium onion, chopped (½ cup)
    1 medium carrot, sliced (½ cup)
    1 bay leaf
    1 teaspoon salt
    ½ teaspoon dried basil, crushed
    ½ teaspoon dried oregano, crushed
    ¼ teaspoon pepper
 1½ cups packaged or frozen noodles
 2½ cups cubed cooked pork

In large kettle combine water, cream-style corn, undrained tomatoes, beef broth, zucchini, onion, carrot, bay leaf, salt, basil, oregano, and pepper. Bring mixture to boiling; reduce heat. Cover and simmer about 5 minutes. Stir in noodles. Cover and simmer about 8 minutes or till noodles are nearly tender. Stir in the cubed pork. Cover and simmer about 5 minutes more or till heated through. Season to taste with salt and pepper. Remove bay leaf. Serves 8.

Honeydew Fruit Salad

    1 honeydew melon
 1½ cups cubed cooked pork or fully
        cooked ham
    1 orange, peeled and sectioned
    ½ cup fresh dark sweet cherries,
        halved and pitted
    ¼ cup chopped celery
    ½ cup peach yogurt
    ¼ cup mayonnaise or salad dressing

Chill all ingredients thoroughly. Cut melon into quarters lengthwise; remove seeds. Starting from one end, cut the fruit from the peel. Cut melon into pieces, leaving pieces in shell. Combine pork or ham, orange sections, cherries, and celery. Toss to mix. Spoon the fruit mixture into melon quarters. Blend peach yogurt and mayonnaise or salad dressing; spoon over fruit mixture on melon. Makes 4 servings.

Pork and Pea Pods

    2 medium onions, cut into thin wedges
    2 tablespoons butter or margarine
    ¾ cup water
    2 tablespoons soy sauce
    2 tablespoons dry sherry
    2 teaspoons instant beef bouillon granules
    1 teaspoon sugar
    ⅛ teaspoon ground ginger
    2 cups cubed cooked pork
    ¼ cup cold water
    4 teaspoons cornstarch
    1 6-ounce package frozen pea pods,
        partially thawed

In 2-quart saucepan cook onion wedges in butter or margarine till tender but not brown. Add ¾ cup water, soy sauce, dry sherry, beef bouillon granules, sugar, and ginger. Stir in pork. Cover and simmer for 10 minutes. Blend the ¼ cup cold water into cornstarch; stir into meat mixture. Cook, stirring constantly, till mixture is thickened and bubbly. Stir in pea pods; cover and simmer for 3 minutes. Transfer to serving dish. Makes 4 servings.

Three creative ways to use cooked pork are Orange-Pork Salad, Barbecued Pork Sandwiches, and Spicy Pork Tacos.

Spicy Pork Tacos

    1 cup chopped onion
    ½ cup chopped celery
    1 clove garlic, minced
    1 tablespoon butter *or* margarine
    1 8-ounce can tomato sauce
    1 4-ounce can green chili peppers, rinsed,
       seeded, and chopped
    ¾ teaspoon chili powder
    ½ teaspoon dried oregano, crushed
    ¼ teaspoon salt
    2 cups chopped cooked pork
       Guacamole
    ½ cup dairy sour cream
    2 cups shredded lettuce
   12 taco shells

In skillet cook onion, celery, and garlic in butter or margarine till tender. Stir in tomato sauce, chili peppers, chili powder, oregano, and salt. Cover and simmer for 5 minutes. Stir in pork; heat through. Keep warm.

Spoon a little Guacamole, sour cream, lettuce, and hot meat mixture into each taco shell; serve immediately. Makes 6 servings.

Guacamole: In a blender container place: 2 medium *avocados*, seeded, peeled, and cut up; ½ small *onion*, cut up; 2 tablespoons *lemon juice*; 1 clove *garlic*, minced; ½ teaspoon *salt*; and ¼ teaspoon *pepper*. Cover; blend till well combined. Makes about 1¼ cups.

Curried Pork

    1 large apple, cored and chopped
    ¼ cup sliced green onion
    2 teaspoons curry powder
    1 tablespoon butter *or* margarine
    1 10¾-ounce can condensed cream of
       mushroom soup
    ¾ cup milk
    2 tablespoons snipped parsley
    2 cups cubed cooked pork
    1 cup dairy sour cream

In saucepan cook chopped apple, green onion, and curry powder in butter or margarine till onion is tender. Stir in soup, milk, and parsley. Add pork; simmer, uncovered, 10 minutes. Stir in sour cream. Heat through, but *do not boil*. Serve over hot, cooked *rice*. Makes 4 servings.

Orange-Pork Salad

    3 tablespoons frozen orange juice
       concentrate, thawed
    3 tablespoons salad oil
    1 tablespoon sugar
    1 tablespoon vinegar
    ⅛ teaspoon dry mustard
       Few drops bottled hot pepper sauce
    ¼ cup mayonnaise *or* salad dressing
    2 cups cubed cooked pork
    1 cup bias-sliced celery
    ½ cup sliced pitted ripe olives
    1 orange
    1 avocado

Stir together orange juice concentrate, oil, sugar, vinegar, mustard, pepper sauce, and dash *salt*. Stir in mayonnaise. Add pork, celery, and olives; toss. Cover and chill. Peel and section orange into bowl, saving any juice. Peel and slice avocado into bowl with orange sections and juices; toss to coat. To serve, mound pork mixture atop lettuce-lined plates. Garnish with drained orange and avocado slices. Sprinkle toasted slivered almonds atop, if desired. Makes 4 servings.

Barbecued Pork Sandwiches

    ½ pound cooked pork
    1 8-ounce can tomato sauce
    ½ cup chopped onion
    ¼ cup finely chopped green pepper
    1 clove garlic, minced
    2 tablespoons vinegar
    1 tablespoon brown sugar
    1 tablespoon worcestershire sauce
   1½ teaspoons dry mustard
    1 teaspoon chili powder
    1 teaspoon dried basil, crushed
    ½ teaspoon paprika
    ¼ teaspoon celery seed
       Dash bottled hot pepper sauce
    4 individual French rolls, split
       Coleslaw (optional)

Cut pork across grain into very thin slices; set aside. In large saucepan combine tomato sauce and next 12 ingredients. Bring to boiling; reduce heat. Cover and simmer for 15 minutes. Add pork. Cover and simmer 15 minutes. Toast rolls. Spoon meat mixture onto bottom half of each roll. Spoon some coleslaw atop meat filling, if desired. Top with other half of roll. Serves 4.

Ham and Bacon

Curing and smoking processes give ham and bacon their distinctive flavor and texture. Ham is classified as "fully cooked" or "cook before eating," depending on the extent of processing. The recipes in this chapter call for fully cooked ham, which is the most readily available. Canned ham is the most popular form of ham sold, but ham also is sold in a wide variety of sizes and shapes, from a whole ham weighing 10 to 18 pounds to smaller cuts such as ham slice, ham cubes, and ground ham. Ham, meaty ham bones, smoked pork hocks, bacon, and Canadian-style bacon are versatile meats, as demonstrated in the following recipe pages. You'll find recipes for omelets, casseroles, sandwiches, and much more using ground or cubed ham; soups and bean dishes using smoked pork hocks and ham bones; and easy ways to dress up canned ham or Canadian-style bacon.

Ham Identification

1 Virginia-Style Ham
2 Country-Style Ham
3 Whole Ham
4 Slab Bacon
5 Ham Rump Portion
6 Ham Shank Portion
7 Semi-Boneless Ham
8 Canned Ham

9 Ham Bone (Meaty)
10 Canadian-Style Bacon
11 Smoked Pork Hocks
12 Boneless Ham
13 Ham Cubes
14 Ham Center Slice
15 Sliced Bacon

Identifying Ham and Bacon

All meat labeled "ham" must come from the hind leg of a pig. It may be fresh, but is usually cured and smoked. Curing may be done by rubbing salt over surface and storing in a cool place; this is called dry salt cure (country-style ham, for example). Another way to cure is by pumping a salt solution (brine) into the meat, leaving it for a certain time, then rinsing it away. After curing, the ham often is smoked and cooked.

When hams are labeled "fully cooked," they are ready to eat but may be heated before serving. When labeled "cook before eating," the ham was not completely cooked during processing and needs further cooking. (See Tip Box below right for further information.)

The term "water added" on the label indicates that the ham has retained water from the curing process and it weighs more after processing than it did before curing. Added moisture cannot exceed 10% of the weight of the fresh ham.

Ham Cuts

Whole Ham: This pear-shaped cut contains the leg and shank bones, and usually weighs 10 to 18 pounds.

Ham Shank Half: Lower half of whole ham; includes the shank bone and part of the leg bone. It has a smaller proportion of meat to bone than rump half. Called *Ham Shank Portion* when center slices are removed.

Ham Rump (Butt) Half: Upper half of whole ham. It has more meat to bone than the shank half. Called *Ham Rump Portion* or *Butt Portion* when center slices are removed.

Ham Center Slice: Oval-shaped, meaty cut from center of whole ham. Contains round leg bone that may be removed for a boneless slice.

Boneless Ham: (Also referred to as a rolled, shaped, formed, or sectioned and formed ham.) Bones and most of the fat are removed; the remaining lean meat often is shaped inside a casing or placed in a can and processed. A whole ham averages 7 to 10 pounds and is usually cut into smaller pieces. Most boneless hams are fully cooked, but some may need additional cooking.

Partially Boned Ham: One or two of the three bones (shank, aitch, and leg) in a whole ham are removed. It's called a *Shankless Ham* when the shank bone is removed, and a *Semi-Boneless Ham* when both the shank and aitch bones are removed. May be fully cooked or may require cooking before eating.

Canned Ham: Usually boneless, cured ham pieces that are placed in a can, then vacuum sealed and fully cooked. A small amount of dry gelatin is added before sealing to absorb the natural ham juices while the ham cooks. The traditional pear-shaped canned hams range in weight from 1½ to 10 pounds. Check label for storage instructions; most need to be refrigerated.

Ham Bone: The bone from any of the ham cuts. Meaty ham bones often are used to add flavor and some meat to soups and stews.

Ham Cubes or Pieces: Cut from any meaty section of the pig's hind leg that has been cured and smoked. Often used for kabobs.

Other Smoked Cuts

Canadian-Style Bacon: A boneless piece of meat from the loin that is shaped into a compact roll, cured, and smoked. It usually should be cooked before eating. Often served sliced.

Slab Bacon: Fresh side pork that has been cured and smoked. It has streaks of lean meat and fat.

Smoked Pork Hocks: (Also called smoked ham hocks.) Hocks that contain shank bones and that are about 2 to 3 inches thick. They are cured and smoked. Often used to add flavor and meat to soups.

Cook-Before-Eating Hams

A label that identifies a ham as "cook before eating" indicates the ham was not completely cooked during processing. Hams are retailed as whole, half, shank, and rump portions. Bake these cook-before-eating hams to an internal temperature of 160°.

You also can buy country or country-style hams that are distinctively flavored and specially processed hams. They are dry-salt cured and, although they may or may not be smoked, they usually are aged. Generally they are saltier than regular hams and often are named for the locality in which they are processed, such as "Smithfield ham," in which case the ham must have been processed within the limits of Smithfield, Virginia.

Follow the label directions for preparing these specialty hams. If desired, use the following information as a guideline for preparing a country-style ham: Thoroughly scrub and rinse a *country-style ham*. Soak in water overnight; drain. Place in a large kettle and cover with water. Bring to boiling. Reduce heat and simmer for about 20 minutes per pound. Remove ham. When ham is just cool enough to handle, remove the skin from it and trim excess fat. Stud the fat side with whole *cloves* and sprinkle with *brown sugar*. Bake in a 350° oven about 20 minutes. Slice thinly. Or, chill the meat after simmering; then follow the chart on page 49 for a fully cooked bone-in ham for the roasting time and temperature.

Baking Ham

Place meat, fat side up, on a rack in a shallow baking pan. If desired, score ham fat in diamond pattern as shown at right. A paper strip makes a handy cutting guide. Make the cuts only about ¼ inch deep.

Insert meat thermometer, placing thermometer so its bulb rests in center of the thickest portion of meat and does not rest in fat or touch bone. Do not add water or other liquid, and do not cover baking pan. (Follow the label directions for heating canned hams.)

Bake the ham in a 325° oven until meat thermome-

ter registers the specified temperature. (Check the label to see whether ham is a fully cooked or a cook-before-eating ham. If not marked, use the cook-before-eating temperatures and times.) Fully cooked and canned hams should be heated to 140° internal temperature and cook-before-eating hams should be baked to an internal tem-

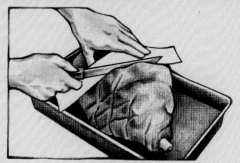

perature of 160°. To check the temperature, push the thermometer into meat a little farther.

If desired, prepare a glaze for the ham. Some suggested glazes are on page 88. To glaze the ham, spoon off fat from baking pan 20 to 30 minutes before end of baking time. Brush glaze over meat. Continue baking and basting with glaze till the thermometer registers the desired internal temperature. Use the baking times below as a guide to total cooking time for a particular type of ham.

Ham Cut	Approximate Weight (pounds)	Internal Temperature of Meat	Approximate Cooking Time (total time)
		Bake meat at constant 325° oven temperature	
Fully Cooked Ham			
whole, bone in	10 to 14	140°	2½ to 3½ hours
half, bone in	5 to 7	140°	1¾ to 2¼ hours
whole, boneless	10 to 12	140°	3 to 3½ hours
half, boneless	5 to 7	140°	2 to 2¼ hours
portion, boneless	3 to 4	140°	1½ to 1¾ hours
whole, semi-boneless	10 to 12	140°	3 to 3½ hours
half, semi-boneless	4 to 6	140°	1¾ to 2½ hours
canned ham	1½ to 3	140°	1 to 1½ hours
	3 to 7	140°	1½ to 2 hours
	7 to 10	140°	2 to 2½ hours
Cook-Before-Eating Ham			
whole	10 to 14	160°	3½ to 4 hours
half	5 to 7	160°	3 to 3¼ hours
shank portion	3 to 4	160°	2 to 2½ hours
rump portion	3 to 4	160°	2 to 2½ hours

Ham

Cherry-Almond-Glazed Ham

If desired, prepare a sauce from page 88 to serve with the leftover ham at another meal —

- 1   **10- to 14-pound fully cooked whole ham**
- 1   **10-ounce jar cherry preserves**
- ¼   **cup red wine vinegar**
- 2   **tablespoons light corn syrup**
- ¼   **teaspoon ground cinnamon**
- ¼   **teaspoon ground nutmeg**
- ¼   **teaspoon ground cloves**
- ⅓   **cup toasted slivered almonds**

Place ham on rack in shallow baking pan. Insert meat thermometer. Bake, uncovered, in 325° oven for 2 to 3 hours.

Meanwhile, for glaze, in a saucepan combine preserves, vinegar, corn syrup, cinnamon, nutmeg, and cloves. Cook and stir till boiling. Reduce heat; simmer 2 minutes. Add almonds. Reserve ¾ cup.

Spoon some of the remaining glaze over ham. Continue baking and basting occasionally with glaze mixture till thermometer registers 140°. Remove from oven; place on a heated serving platter. Add 3 tablespoons *water* to reserved ¾ cup glaze; heat and pass. Serves 20 to 25.

Plum-Orange Sauced Ham

- 1   **5- to 7-pound fully cooked ham shank portion**
- ⅓   **cup honey**
- 2   **tablespoons soy sauce**
- 2   **tablespoons lemon juice**
-     **Plum-Orange Sauce**

Place ham on rack in shallow baking pan. Insert meat thermometer. Bake, uncovered, in a 325° oven for 1½ to 1¾ hours or till meat thermometer registers 130°. Stir together honey, soy, and lemon juice; baste ham with mixture. Continue baking and basting occasionally till thermometer registers 140°. Serve with Plum-Orange Sauce. Serves 12 to 16.

Plum-Orange Sauce: Drain one 16-ounce can whole, unpitted *purple plums,* reserving ¼ cup syrup. Remove pits and force plums through sieve. In saucepan combine sieved plums, reserved syrup, ¼ teaspoon finely shredded *orange peel,* 3 tablespoons *orange juice,* 2 tablespoons *sugar,* ½ teaspoon *worcestershire sauce,* and ¼ teaspoon ground *cinnamon.* Bring to boiling; reduce heat. Cover and simmer 10 minutes.

Sweet-Sour Ham

You can prepare this barbecued ham even if your grill doesn't have a spit attachment. Just follow directions in note at end of recipe —

- 1   **5-pound fully cooked canned ham**
- 1   **20-ounce can pineapple slices**
- ¼   **cup dry sherry *or* dry white wine**
- 3   **tablespoons vinegar**
- 2   **tablespoons soy sauce**
- 2   **tablespoons honey**
- 1   **tablespoon cooking oil**
- 1   **clove garlic, minced**
-     **Dash salt**
- 2   **small green peppers, cut into 1½-inch squares**
- 12 **cherry tomatoes**
- 2   **limes, cut into wedges**

Insert spit rod through center of ham. Adjust holding forks; test balance. In covered grill place *medium* coals on both sides of drip pan. Attach spit; position drip pan under meat. Insert meat thermometer. Turn on motor; lower grill hood or cover with foil tent. Grill ham over *medium* coals about 1 hour.

Meanwhile, for sauce, drain pineapple, reserving ⅔ cup syrup. Set drained pineapple aside. In saucepan combine the reserved syrup, dry sherry, vinegar, soy sauce, honey, cooking oil, garlic, and salt. Boil mixture down to ⅔ cup (about 10 minutes); stir occasionally.

Brush ham with sauce. Continue baking and basting occasionally with sauce about 30 minutes or till thermometer registers 140°. Pass remaining sauce. Before serving, quarter each pineapple slice. Thread 12 small bamboo skewers with green pepper squares, pieces of pineapple, cherry tomato, and lime wedges. Serve with ham. Makes 12 servings.

Note: If grill does not have spit, place ham directly on grill over drip pan. Lower hood, or tent grill with heavy-duty foil. Grill ham over *medium* coals for 1 hour. Lift foil tent; turn ham. Insert meat thermometer; brush ham with sauce. Re-cover grill with foil tent. Continue baking and basting occasionally with sauce about 30 minutes or till thermometer registers 140°.

Scandinavian Jul Ham

1 3- to 4-pound fully cooked boneless ham
2 egg whites
2 tablespoons sugar
2 tablespoons dry mustard
⅓ to ½ cup fine dry bread crumbs

Trim fat from ham; place ham on rack in shallow baking pan. Insert meat thermometer. Bake, uncovered, in 325° oven about 1¼ hours. Combine egg whites, sugar, and mustard. Brush *half* of the mixture over top and sides of ham. Sprinkle with *half* of the bread crumbs, patting them on the ham's sides. Repeat with remaining egg white mixture and crumbs. Bake ham 15 to 20 minutes more or till thermometer registers 140°. Serve ham hot or cold. Makes 10 to 12 servings.

Planked Ham

1 3-pound fully cooked canned ham
1½ teaspoons finely shredded orange peel
½ cup orange juice
¼ cup light corn syrup
5 hot cooked sweet potatoes, peeled
1 egg
3 tablespoons butter *or* margarine
1 teaspoon salt
½ teaspoon ground nutmeg
   Cooking oil
1 orange

Place ham on rack in shallow baking pan. Bake, uncovered, in 325° oven for 35 minutes. Meanwhile, for glaze combine ½ *teaspoon* of the orange peel, orange juice, and corn syrup. Bring to boiling. Spoon some glaze over ham; continue baking 20 to 25 minutes, basting occasionally with glaze. In bowl beat together potatoes, the remaining 1 teaspoon orange peel, the egg, *1 tablespoon* of the butter, salt, and nutmeg. If necessary, add a little orange juice to soften sweet potatoes. Place ham on a seasoned plank or wooden board. Using pastry bag with large star tip, pipe border of sweet potatoes around ham. Melt the remaining 2 tablespoons butter; drizzle over potatoes. Brush exposed wood with oil. Peel and slice orange; cut slices in half and arrange atop ham. Brush with remaining glaze. Return to oven; bake about 30 minutes or till a meat thermometer registers 140°. Serves 10.

Note: To season a non-varnished wooden plank, brush it with cooking oil and heat it in a 325° oven about 1 hour.

Apricot-Wine Glazed Ham

Shown on the cover—

1 5- to 7-pound fully cooked ham rump (butt) portion
24 whole cloves
¼ cup dry white wine
2 tablespoons lemon juice
2 teaspoons cornstarch
⅓ cup apricot preserves *or* seedless red raspberry jam
1 tablespoon butter *or* margarine
   Watercress (optional)
   Spiced crab apples (optional)

Score ham using a sharp knife to make shallow cuts diagonally across ham in a diamond pattern. Stud with cloves. Place ham on rack in shallow baking pan. Insert meat thermometer. Bake, uncovered, in 325° oven for 1¾ to 2¼ hours or till meat thermometer registers 140°.

Meanwhile, for glaze, in a small saucepan blend wine and lemon juice into cornstarch. Add about *half* of the preserves or jam. Cook and stir till thickened and bubbly. Stir in the remaining preserves or jam and butter or margarine. Heat and stir till butter is melted. Brush ham with some of the glaze. Bake ham 10 minutes more. Spoon any remaining glaze over ham. Garnish platter using watercress and spiced crab apples, if desired. Makes 12 to 16 servings.

Honey and Spice Ham

1 4- to 5-pound fully cooked semi-boneless ham half
¼ cup honey
2 tablespoons butter *or* margarine
⅛ teaspoon ground cinnamon
⅛ teaspoon ground turmeric
   Dash ground cloves

Place ham on rack in shallow baking pan. Insert meat thermometer. Bake in 325° oven about 1½ hours. In small saucepan combine honey, butter or margarine, cinnamon, turmeric, and cloves. Cook and stir till mixture is bubbly. Spoon mixture over ham and continue baking 20 to 30 minutes more or till meat thermometer registers 140°. Makes 12 servings.

To prepare Ham en Croûte, use a canned ham; for the Sherried Ham-Fruit Kabobs, use fully cooked ham cubes.

Ham en Croûte

1 5-pound fully cooked canned ham
2 cups chopped fresh mushrooms
¼ cup sliced green onion
1 clove garlic, minced
2 tablespoons butter *or* margarine
¼ cup fine dry bread crumbs
2 tablespoons grated parmesan cheese
2 tablespoons dry white wine
1 tablespoon snipped parsley
1½ cups all-purpose flour
2 teaspoons baking powder
½ teaspoon ground sage
½ teaspoon dry mustard
¼ cup shortening
½ cup milk
1 beaten egg
Watercress
Preserved kumquats

Place ham on rack in shallow baking pan. Insert meat thermometer. Bake in 325° oven for 1½ to 2 hours or till meat thermometer registers 140°. Remove ham from oven; remove drippings from pan using baster. Remove rack. Cool ham 20 minutes. Trim any excess fat from outside of ham.

While ham is baking prepare the filling. In saucepan cook mushrooms, green onion, and garlic in butter or margarine about 3 minutes; remove from heat. In a bowl combine the mushroom mixture, dry bread crumbs, parmesan cheese, wine, and parsley. Cover and chill at least 1 hour in the refrigerator.

To make pastry, stir together flour, baking powder, sage, and dry mustard. Cut in shortening till pieces are the size of small peas. Gradually add the ½ cup milk, 1 tablespoon at a time, tossing with a fork till all is moistened; form pastry into a ball.

On a lightly floured surface, roll out pastry to 14x12-inch rectangle. Spread chilled mushroom filling atop the ham. Drape the pastry over ham, according to directions in tip box at right. Trim. Make slits in top. Cut decorations from the remaining dough and arrange over the top.

Brush pastry with the beaten egg. Bake in 450° oven for 10 to 15 minutes or till pastry is browned. Transfer to serving platter. Garnish with sprigs of watercress and preserved kumquats. Makes 12 to 15 servings.

Sherried Ham-Fruit Kabobs

1 8¼-ounce can pineapple slices
½ cup apricot preserves
⅓ cup cream sherry
2 tablespoons light corn syrup
1 tablespoon lemon juice
⅛ teaspoon ground cinnamon
Dash ground cloves
1½ pounds fully cooked boneless ham, cut into 1-inch cubes
2 oranges, each cut into 6 wedges
2 firm medium pears, peeled, cored, and quartered
1 16-ounce jar spiced crab apples

Drain pineapple slices, reserving ¼ cup syrup. Halve each pineapple slice and set aside. For the sauce, in saucepan stir together the reserved pineapple syrup, apricot preserves, sherry, corn syrup, lemon juice, cinnamon, cloves, and dash *salt*. Bring to boiling, stirring frequently. Reduce heat and simmer, uncovered, for 1 minute, stirring once or twice. Preheat the broiler.

On 6 skewers thread ham cubes, pineapple pieces, orange wedges, and pear quarters. Place kabobs on unheated rack of broiler pan. Broil 4 inches from heat for 10 minutes, turning frequently and brushing with the sauce. Thread crab apples onto the ends of skewers. Broil kabobs for 5 to 10 minutes more, turning often and brushing with sauce. Serves 6.

Covering Ham with Pastry

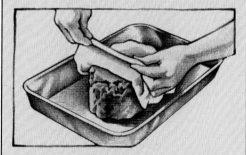

Place baked ham in pan without a rack. Roll out pastry; drape over mushroom-topped ham, covering top and sides with pastry. Mold pastry to the shape of the meat. Trim off extra pastry at bottom; cut slits in top. Decorate with pastry cutouts. Brush with egg.

Wilted Spinach-Ham Toss

½ pound fresh spinach
  Whole black pepper
1 *or* 2 slices bacon
1 tablespoon white wine vinegar
2 teaspoons lemon juice
½ teaspoon sugar
¼ teaspoon salt
1½ cups fully cooked ham cut into thin
    strips
1 cup sliced fresh mushrooms
¼ cup sliced green onion
2 hard-cooked eggs, chopped

Wash spinach and pat dry on paper toweling. Tear spinach into bite-size pieces (totals about 6 cups) and place in a mixing bowl. Grind a generous amount of pepper over the spinach. Set aside.

Cut uncooked bacon into small pieces. In large skillet cook bacon till crisp. Stir in vinegar, lemon juice, sugar, and salt. Gradually add ham, mushrooms, and green onion to the skillet mixture; stir constantly. Remove from heat; add spinach. Using two spoons or forks, toss the spinach mixture to coat evenly with ham mixture. Turn spinach mixture into serving dish. Sprinkle with chopped, hard-cooked eggs and serve immediately. Makes 4 servings.

Potato-Ham Scallop

2 cups cubed fully cooked ham
6 to 8 medium potatoes, peeled and thinly
    sliced (6 cups)
¼ cup finely chopped onion
⅓ cup all-purpose flour
2 cups milk
3 tablespoons fine dry bread crumbs
1 tablespoon butter *or* margarine, melted
2 tablespoons finely snipped parsley

Place *half* the ham in a 2-quart casserole. Cover with *half* the potatoes and *half* the onion. Sift *half* the flour over; season with salt and pepper. Repeat layering ham, potatoes, and onion. Season with additional salt and pepper. Sift remaining flour atop. Pour milk over all.

Bake, covered, in 350° oven for 1¼ to 1½ hours or till potatoes are nearly tender. Uncover. Combine bread crumbs and melted butter; sprinkle atop casserole. Top with parsley. Bake 15 minutes more. Makes 6 to 8 servings.

Molded Ham-Potato Salad

1 envelope unflavored gelatin
¼ cup cold water
1 10¾-ounce can condensed cream of
    potato soup
¼ cup milk
½ cup dairy sour cream
1½ teaspoons prepared mustard
1 teaspoon lemon juice
1 cup finely chopped fully cooked ham
½ cup chopped celery
3 tablespoons sliced green onion
2 tablespoons chopped pimiento
¼ teaspoon dried dillweed
  Lettuce

Soften unflavored gelatin in cold water. In saucepan combine soup, milk, and softened gelatin. Stir over low heat till gelatin is dissolved. Remove from heat; stir in sour cream, mustard, and lemon juice. Chill gelatin mixture till partially set. Fold in ham, celery, green onion, pimiento, and dillweed. Turn into an oiled 8x4x2-inch loaf pan. Chill 4 to 5 hours or overnight. Unmold onto lettuce-lined platter. Garnish with hard-cooked egg slices and parsley, if desired. Serves 6.

Stuffed Pepper Salad

2 cups shredded cabbage
1 cup chopped fully cooked ham
½ cup coarsely shredded carrot
¼ cup sliced radish
¼ cup chopped cucumber
1 8-ounce carton plain yogurt
2 teaspoons sugar
1 teaspoon lemon juice
½ teaspoon celery seed
¼ teaspoon garlic salt
¼ teaspoon onion salt
  Dash freshly ground black pepper
2 large green peppers

In bowl combine shredded cabbage, ham, carrot, radish, and cucumber. Combine yogurt, sugar, lemon juice, celery seed, garlic salt, onion salt, and pepper; mix well. Pour over vegetable mixture, tossing to coat. Cover and chill mixture at least 1 hour.

Remove tops from green peppers. Cut peppers in half lengthwise and remove seeds. Spoon vegetable mixture into pepper cups. If desired, garnish with more sliced radish or chopped, hard-cooked egg. Makes 4 servings.

Brussels Sprouts and Ham

1 **10-ounce package frozen brussels sprouts**
¼ **cup chopped onion**
3 **tablespoons butter *or* margarine**
2 **tablespoons all-purpose flour**
½ **teaspoon dried marjoram, crushed**
1¾ **cups milk**
½ **cup shredded American cheese (2 ounces)**
2 **cups cubed fully cooked ham**
1½ **cups herb-seasoned stuffing mix**
1 **tablespoon butter *or* margarine**

Cook brussels sprouts according to package directions. Drain; halve any large sprouts and set aside all sprouts. Cook onion in 3 tablespoons butter or margarine till tender but not brown. Blend in flour and marjoram. Add milk all at once. Cook and stir till thickened and bubbly. Stir in cheese. Stir in ham, *1 cup* of the stuffing mix, and brussels sprouts. Turn into a 1½-quart casserole. Melt remaining 1 tablespoon butter; toss with remaining ½ cup stuffing mix. Sprinkle atop casserole. Bake, uncovered, in 350° oven for 25 minutes. Makes 4 to 6 servings.

Microwave directions: In a 1½-quart non-metal casserole combine brussels sprouts and 2 tablespoons *water*. Cover with lid, waxed paper, or clear plastic wrap. Cook in countertop microwave oven on high power for 7 minutes, stirring once. Drain; halve any large sprouts and set aside all sprouts. In same casserole micro-cook onion and the 3 tablespoons butter, covered, on high for 2 minutes. Blend in flour and marjoram; add milk all at once. Micro-cook, uncovered, about 6 minutes or till thickened and bubbly, stirring after every minute. Add cheese; stir till melted. Stir in ham, *1 cup* of the stuffing mix, and brussels sprouts. In small non-metal bowl melt the remaining 1 tablespoon butter or margarine on high for 30 to 45 seconds; toss with remaining ½ cup stuffing mix. Sprinkle atop casserole. Micro-cook, uncovered, for 5 to 6 minutes or till heated through, giving dish a half turn once. Makes 4 to 6 servings.

Cheesy Beer-Ham Soup

3 **medium potatoes, peeled and cut up (3 cups)**
1 **small onion, finely chopped (⅓ cup)**
2 **cups water**
1 **teaspoon instant chicken bouillon granules**
1 **17-ounce can whole kernel corn**
1 **cup beer**
1 **4-ounce can mushroom stems and pieces**
2 **tablespoons snipped parsley**
½ **teaspoon dry mustard**
⅓ **cup cold water**
2 **tablespoons all-purpose flour**
2 **cups shredded American cheese (8 ounces)**
2 **cups cubed fully cooked ham**

In 3-quart saucepan combine potatoes and onion; add the 2 cups water. Bring to boiling; stir in bouillon granules. Cover and cook about 20 minutes or till potatoes are tender. Stir in *undrained* corn, beer, *undrained* mushrooms, parsley, and dry mustard. Bring to boiling. Reduce heat; cover and simmer 15 minutes.

Blend cold water into flour. Stir into hot vegetable mixture. Cook and stir till slightly thickened and bubbly. Stir in the shredded cheese and ham. Continue heating and stirring till cheese is melted. Makes 6 servings.

Ham and Egg Bake

⅓ **cup sliced green onion**
¼ **cup butter *or* margarine**
¼ **cup all-purpose flour**
1 **teaspoon dry mustard**
¼ **teaspoon salt**
⅛ **teaspoon pepper**
2 **cups milk**
8 **hard-cooked eggs, sliced**
2 **cups chopped fully cooked ham**
¼ **cup grated parmesan cheese**
   Paprika

Cook green onion in butter or margarine till tender but not brown. Blend in flour, mustard, salt, and pepper; add milk all at once. Cook and stir till thickened and bubbly. In bottom of an 8x1½-inch round baking dish arrange *half* of the egg slices; top with *half* of the ham. Repeat layers. Pour sauce mixture over all. Sprinkle with cheese and paprika. Bake, uncovered, in 350° oven for 25 to 30 minutes. Serves 4 to 6.

Ham Slices

Layered Ham Florentine

2 ¾- to 1-pound fully cooked ham center
   slices, cut ½ inch thick
2 10-ounce packages frozen chopped
   spinach, thawed and drained
¼ cup finely chopped onion
¼ cup finely snipped parsley
½ cup dairy sour cream
½ cup mayonnaise *or* salad dressing
1 tablespoon prepared mustard

Slash edge of each ham slice to prevent curling.
Place one of the slices on rack in shallow baking
pan. Combine spinach, onion, and parsley;
spoon atop ham slice, spreading mixture almost
to edges. Place remaining ham slice atop
spinach mixture. Bake in 350° oven for 35 to 40
minutes or till heated through. In saucepan
combine sour cream, mayonnaise, and mustard;
heat through but *do not boil*. Cut ham stack into
slices to serve. Spoon mustard mixture over individual servings. Makes 6 servings.

Ham Caribbean

1 2-pound fully cooked ham center slice,
   cut 1 inch thick
2 oranges
  Orange juice
1 tablespoon whole cloves
⅓ cup packed brown sugar
4 teaspoons cornstarch
2 tablespoons rum
1 tablespoon honey
1 8¼-ounce can pineapple chunks, drained
½ cup light raisins

Slash edge of ham slice; place on rack in shallow baking pan. Bake in 350° oven for 30 minutes. Meanwhile, peel and section oranges over
bowl to catch juice. Set orange sections aside.
Measure juice in bowl; add additional orange
juice if necessary to make ⅓ cup liquid. In
saucepan combine orange juice and whole
cloves; bring to boiling. Simmer gently, uncovered, for 5 minutes; discard cloves. Combine
brown sugar and cornstarch; blend in rum and
honey. Stir mixture into orange juice. Cook and
stir till thickened and bubbly. Stir in orange sections, pineapple chunks, and raisins. Heat
through. Spoon over ham. Makes 6 servings.

Ham Slice with Curried Fruit

1 8¾-ounce can peach slices
1 8½-ounce can pear halves
1 8¼-ounce can pineapple chunks
1 2-pound fully cooked ham center slice,
   cut 1 inch thick
2 tablespoons butter *or* margarine
2 tablespoons brown sugar
1 to 1½ teaspoons curry powder
½ of a 16-ounce can pitted dark sweet
   cherries

Drain peaches, pears, and pineapple; reserve a
total of ¾ cup of the fruit liquid. Slash edge of
ham slice; place on rack in shallow baking pan.
Pour ¼ cup of the reserved fruit liquid over ham
slice. Bake in 350° oven for 35 minutes, occasionally spooning an additional ¼ *cup* of the remaining fruit liquid over ham.
  In skillet melt butter; stir in brown sugar, the
remaining ¼ cup fruit liquid, and the curry powder. Cut pear halves in half. Add peaches,
pears, and pineapple to butter mixture. Cover;
cook over low heat 15 minutes, stirring occasionally. Drain cherries; rinse if desired, and
carefully stir into fruit mixture. Cook 10 minutes
more. Transfer ham to serving platter; spoon fruit
mixture over ham. Makes 6 servings.

Grilled Ham Slice with Chili-Plum Sauce

¼ cup sliced green onion
3 tablespoons butter *or* margarine
½ cup plum jam
¼ cup chili sauce
2 tablespoons dry white wine
1½ teaspoons lemon juice
½ teaspoon ground allspice
1 2-pound fully cooked ham center slice,
   cut 1 inch thick
1 tablespoon snipped parsley

In saucepan cook green onion in butter or margarine till tender but not brown; add plum jam,
chili sauce, wine, lemon juice, and allspice.
Bring to boiling; reduce heat. Simmer, uncovered, 10 minutes, stirring occasionally. Keep
sauce warm. Slash fat edge of ham slice. Grill
ham slice over *medium* coals about 15 minutes.
Brush with sauce. Turn ham; brush sauce over
ham. Grill 10 to 15 minutes more. Spoon sauce
over ham before serving. Sprinkle ham with
parsley. Serves 6.

Peaches, pears, pineapple, and cherries combine to make a refreshing entrée in Ham Slice with Curried Fruit.

Burgundied Ham Veronique

2 tablespoons butter *or* margarine
2 tablespoons sugar
   Dash ground ginger
1 2½- to 3-pound fully cooked ham center
      slice, cut 1½ inches thick
2 tablespoons chopped green onion
1 cup burgundy
2 tablespoons cold water
4 teaspoons cornstarch
1 cup seedless green grapes *or* seeded
      Tokay grapes, halved

In large skillet melt butter; stir in sugar and
ginger. Brown ham quickly on both sides in
butter-sugar mixture. Remove ham from skillet.
Cook onion in drippings over low heat till tender
but not brown. Stir in burgundy; bring to boiling.
Blend water into cornstarch; add to burgundy
mixture. Cook and stir till thickened and bubbly.
Return ham to skillet; spoon sauce over ham.
Cover and simmer for 15 minutes. Add grapes;
cook 1 to 2 minutes more. Transfer ham to warm
platter; spoon some sauce and grapes atop.
Pass remaining sauce. Makes 6 servings.

Microwave directions: Place ham in a
12x7½x2-inch baking dish. Cook in countertop
microwave oven on high power about 15 minutes or till heated through, giving dish a half turn
after 8 minutes. Drain; cover and set aside. In a
4-cup glass measure combine sugar, ginger,
and cornstarch; stir in burgundy, water, onion,
and butter. Micro-cook, uncovered, 2 minutes or
till thickened and bubbly, stirring after each
minute. Stir in grapes. Return to microwave oven
and cook on high power for 1 minute. Transfer
ham to warm serving platter; spoon some sauce
and grapes atop. Pass remaining sauce.

Hamwiches

¼ cup mayonnaise *or* salad dressing
1 teaspoon bottled steak sauce
½ teaspoon minced dried onion
6 slices Swiss cheese
6 thin slices fully cooked ham
1 large dill pickle, cut into 6 strips
6 hard rolls, split

Combine mayonnaise, steak sauce, and onion.
Place a cheese slice atop each ham slice;
spread with mayonnaise mixture. Place a pickle
strip across end of each cheese slice. Roll up;
place in split rolls. Place on baking sheet. Bake
in 400° oven for 8 to 10 minutes. Serves 6.

Breakfast Wheels

   Butter *or* margarine
   Currant jelly
2 English muffins, split and toasted
4 thin slices fully cooked ham
1 large apple, peeled, cored, and thinly
      sliced
4 slices Swiss cheese

Spread butter and jelly on muffin halves. Place a
ham slice, 2 or 3 apple slices, and a cheese
slice atop each half. Broil 4 inches from heat for
3 to 4 minutes or till cheese is melted and lightly
browned. Makes 4 sandwiches.

Microwave directions: Spread butter and
jelly on muffin halves; set aside. Place ham
slices in a 10x6x2-inch non-metal baking dish;
top each with 2 or 3 apple slices. Cook, covered
with waxed paper, in countertop microwave
oven on high power for 1 to 1½ minutes or till
hot. Uncover; top each with a cheese slice.
Micro-cook about 1 minute or till cheese melts.
Place atop muffins.

Ham and Cheese Squares

1 13¾-ounce package hot roll mix
1 cup warm water (110° to 115°)
3 tablespoons prepared mustard
8 ounces fully cooked ham, thinly sliced
1½ cups shredded natural Swiss cheese
      (6 ounces)
½ cup finely chopped onion
1 teaspoon poppy seed
2 teaspoons cooking oil
   Poppy seed

Dissolve yeast from roll mix in the water. Stir in
flour from roll mix. Divide dough in half; set aside
one half of dough and keep covered. On lightly
floured surface roll remaining half of dough to
13x9-inch rectangle. Place in greased 13x9x2-
inch baking pan. Cover; let rise 20 minutes.
Bake in 375° oven for 10 minutes. Remove from
oven. Spread with mustard. Top with *half* of the
sliced ham, all of the cheese and onion; end with
remaining ham. Sprinkle 1 teaspoon poppy
seed over ham. Roll remaining dough to 13x9-
inch rectangle. Place over ham-cheese filling.
Crimp edges. Cover; let rest 10 to 15 minutes.
Brush with cooking oil. Sprinkle additional
poppy seed atop. Bake in 375° oven for 30 to 35
minutes, or till done. To serve, cut into squares.
Makes 6 servings.

Ground Ham

Ham-Noodle Casserole

- 3 ounces medium noodles
- 1 11-ounce can condensed cheddar cheese soup
- ½ cup milk
- ½ cup dairy sour cream
- 1 2½-ounce can sliced mushrooms, drained
- ½ cup thinly sliced celery
- 2 tablespoons chopped pimiento
- 1 tablespoon snipped parsley
- 2 cups ground fully cooked ham
- ¾ cup rich round cracker crumbs
- 1 tablespoon butter *or* margarine, melted

Cook noodles in boiling, unsalted water till tender; drain. In large bowl stir together soup, milk, and sour cream. Add mushrooms, celery, pimiento, and parsley. Stir in cooked noodles and ham. Turn mixture into 2-quart casserole. Combine rich round cracker crumbs and melted butter; sprinkle over casserole. Bake, uncovered, in 375° oven 30 to 35 minutes, or till heated through. Makes 4 to 6 servings.

Microwave directions: Prepare casserole as directed above, *except* do not sprinkle with crumbs. Cook, covered, in countertop microwave oven on high power for about 16 minutes or till heated through, stirring once. Stir before serving; sprinkle with buttered cracker crumbs.

Ham-Yam Bake

- 2 beaten eggs
- ½ cup milk
- ½ cup finely chopped onion
- ½ cup crushed saltine crackers (14 crackers)
- 1 tablespoon horseradish mustard
- 1 pound ground fully cooked ham
- 1 pound ground pork
- 1 17-ounce can (vacuum packed) sweet potatoes, cut into chunks
- ½ cup orange marmalade
- ⅛ teaspoon ground cloves

Combine eggs, milk, onion, crushed crackers, and mustard. Add meats; mix well. Pat into an 8x8x2-inch baking dish. Cover. Bake in 350° oven for 1¼ hours. Drain off excess fat. Arrange sweet potatoes atop meat; drizzle with a mixture of marmalade and cloves. Bake, uncovered, 15 minutes more. Makes 8 or 9 servings.

Ham-Cauliflower Crepes

- 1 10-ounce package frozen cauliflower
- ¼ cup butter *or* margarine
- ¼ cup all-purpose flour
- 2 cups light cream
- ¼ cup dry white wine
- ¼ cup crumbled blue cheese
- 1½ cups ground fully cooked ham
- 1 2-ounce can chopped mushrooms, drained
- 2 tablespoons snipped parsley
- 2 tablespoons milk
- 12 Crepes

Prepare cauliflower according to package directions, cooking only till crisp-tender; drain and set aside. In saucepan melt butter or margarine; blend in flour. Stir in cream; cook and stir till thickened and bubbly. Add wine and cheese; stir till cheese melts. Remove from heat. Slice cauliflower; mix with ham, mushrooms, parsley, and ¾ *cup* of the cheese sauce. Add milk to remaining sauce; cover and set aside. Spoon about ¼ cup ham filling in center of each crepe; overlap edges. Place, seam side down, in greased 13x9x2-inch baking dish. Cover with foil. Bake in 375° oven for 20 minutes. To serve, warm sauce and spoon over crepes. Makes 6 servings.

Crepes: In a bowl combine 1 cup all-purpose *flour*, 1½ cups *milk*, 2 *eggs*, 1 tablespoon *cooking oil*, and ¼ teaspoon *salt*. Beat with rotary beater until blended. Heat a lightly greased 6-inch skillet. Remove from heat; spoon in about 2 tablespoons batter. Lift and tilt skillet to spread batter evenly. Return to heat; brown on one side only. To remove, invert pan over paper toweling; remove crepe. Repeat with remaining batter, greasing skillet occasionally. Makes 16 to 18 crepes.

Freshly Ground Ham

Use your food processor or blender to make ground ham. For the food processor, place steel blade in work bowl. Using knife cut ham into 1-inch pieces. Place up to 1 cup ham pieces in work bowl. Process with on/off turns. For the blender, use knife to cut ham into ½-inch pieces. Place ½ cup ham pieces in blender container. Process till finely chopped.

At your next brunch serve Ham Omelet, which is complemented by a sour cream and cheese sauce.

Ham Omelet

2 tablespoons chopped onion
2 tablespoons chopped green pepper
6 tablespoons butter *or* margarine
⅔ cup ground fully cooked ham
1 3-ounce can sliced mushrooms, drained
1 teaspoon dijon-style mustard
4 egg yolks
4 egg whites
2 tablespoons water
¼ teaspoon salt
2 tablespoons all-purpose flour
¼ teaspoon salt
    Dash pepper
1 cup milk
½ cup shredded Swiss cheese
¼ cup dairy sour cream

In saucepan cook onion and green pepper in *2 tablespoons* of the butter till tender but not brown. Stir in ham, mushrooms, and mustard; heat through over low heat and keep warm.

In small mixer bowl beat egg yolks at high speed of electric mixer about 5 minutes or till thick and lemon-colored. Thoroughly wash beaters. In large mixer bowl beat egg whites till frothy. Add water and ¼ teaspoon salt; continue beating till stiff peaks form. Fold egg yolks into egg whites. In a 10-inch skillet with an oven-proof handle heat *2 tablespoons* of the butter or margarine. Pour in the egg mixture, mounding it slightly higher at the sides. Cook over low heat about 8 minutes or till eggs are puffed and set and bottom is golden brown. Place skillet in 325° oven; bake about 10 minutes or till knife inserted near center comes out clean.

Meanwhile, in small saucepan melt remaining *2 tablespoons* butter or margarine. Blend in flour, ¼ teaspoon salt, and pepper. Add the milk all at once. Cook and stir over medium heat till thickened and bubbly. Cook and stir 2 minutes more. Add cheese; stir till melted and well blended. Remove from heat; gradually stir mixture into sour cream. Blend ¼ cup cheese sauce into the warm ham mixture. Loosen sides of omelet using spatula. Make shallow cut across omelet slightly above and parallel to skillet handle so that the two portions are unequal. Spread ham mixture on larger half. Tilt pan. Fold smaller half over larger half. Using spatula slip omelet onto hot platter. Spoon some cheese sauce atop. If desired, garnish with snipped chives. Pass remaining sauce. Serves 4.

Apricot-Ham Patties

2 beaten eggs
¾ cup milk
1½ cups soft bread crumbs
½ cup finely snipped dried apricots
¼ cup chopped onion
2 tablespoons snipped parsley
1 pound ground fully cooked ham
1 pound ground pork
⅓ cup packed brown sugar
1 teaspoon all-purpose flour

Combine eggs, milk, bread crumbs, dried apricots, onion, parsley, and dash *pepper*. Add ground ham and pork; mix well. Shape meat into 8 patties. Combine brown sugar and flour; sprinkle in bottom of 15x10x1-inch baking pan. Place patties in pan. Bake in 350° oven for 40 to 45 minutes. Transfer patties to serving platter. Stir pan juices and spoon over meat. Serves 8.

Ham Croquettes with Cheese Sauce

3 tablespoons butter *or* margarine
¼ to ½ teaspoon curry powder
¼ cup all-purpose flour
¾ cup milk
2 cups coarsely ground fully cooked ham
2 teaspoons prepared mustard
1 teaspoon grated onion
⅔ cup fine dry bread crumbs
1 beaten egg
2 tablespoons water
    Cooking oil for deep-fat frying
    Cheese Sauce

In saucepan melt butter with curry powder; blend in flour. Add milk all at once; cook and stir till thickened and bubbly. Cook and stir 2 minutes more. Remove from heat. Stir in ham, mustard, and onion. Chill thoroughly. Shape mixture into 10 cones. Roll in bread crumbs, handling lightly. Dip into mixture of egg and water; roll in crumbs again. Fry in deep hot fat (365°) about 2 to 2½ minutes or till golden. Drain. Serve with Cheese Sauce. Makes 5 servings.

Cheese Sauce: In saucepan melt 2 tablespoons *butter or margarine*. Blend in 2 tablespoons all-purpose *flour,* ¼ teaspoon *salt,* and dash *pepper*. Add 1¼ cups *milk* all at once. Cook and stir till thickened and bubbly. Cook and stir 2 minutes more. Stir in ½ cup shredded *American cheese* and ½ cup shredded *Swiss cheese*. Stir till smooth, and cheese is melted.

Ham Mousse

 1 envelope unflavored gelatin
 ⅔ cup chicken broth
 1 beaten egg
 ¼ cup mayonnaise *or* salad dressing
 1 tablespoon chopped green onion
 2 teaspoons dijon-style mustard
 1½ cups ground fully cooked ham
 ½ cup whipping cream

Soften gelatin in ½ cup cold *water;* set aside. Combine chicken broth and beaten egg. Cook and stir over low heat about 7 minutes or till slightly thickened. Add softened gelatin; stir till dissolved. Beat in mayonnaise, onion, and mustard. Add ham. Chill till partially set. Whip cream to soft peaks; fold into ham mixture. Turn mixture into 5 or 6 individual molds. Chill till set. Unmold; serve on lettuce-lined plates, if desired. Makes 5 or 6 servings.

Ham and Cabbage Rolls

 ⅓ cup long grain rice
 2 teaspoons instant chicken bouillon
    granules
 2 beaten eggs
 ¼ cup finely chopped onion
 ¼ cup finely chopped green pepper
 ¼ teaspoon dried thyme, crushed
 ¼ teaspoon dried savory, crushed
 3 cups ground fully cooked ham
 12 large cabbage leaves
 1 cup dairy sour cream
 2 tablespoons all-purpose flour

In saucepan bring rice, *1 teaspoon* of the bouillon granules, and 1 cup *water* to boiling. Reduce heat; cover and simmer about 20 minutes or till done. Combine cooked rice, the eggs, onion, green pepper, thyme, savory, ¼ teaspoon *salt,* and dash *pepper.* Add ham; mix well.

Cut about 2 inches of heavy center vein out of each cabbage leaf. Immerse leaves in boiling water about 3 minutes or just till limp; drain. Place about ¼ cup of the meat mixture in center of each leaf; fold in sides. Fold ends so they overlap atop meat mixture. Place, seam side down, in 10-inch skillet. Dissolve *1 teaspoon* bouillon granules in 1 cup hot *water;* pour over cabbage rolls. Cover and simmer about 25 minutes. Remove to warm platter; keep warm. Combine sour cream and flour; stir into pan juices. Cook and stir till bubbly. Spoon over cabbage rolls. Makes 6 servings.

Mini Ham-Apple Loaves

 ¾ cup finely chopped, peeled cooking
    apple
 ¼ cup chopped onion
 2 tablespoons butter *or* margarine
 2 beaten eggs
 ¼ cup apple juice *or* milk
 1 8-ounce can tomato sauce
 ¾ cup crushed rich round crackers
 1 pound ground fully cooked ham
 1 pound ground pork
 1 tablespoon brown sugar
 1 teaspoon worcestershire sauce

Cook apple and onion in butter till tender. Combine eggs, apple juice, and ¼ *cup* of the tomato sauce; stir in crackers and apple mixture. Add ham and pork; mix well. Pack mixture into six 4-inch individual fluted tube pans (six to a pan). Place on shallow baking pan. Bake in 350° oven about 30 minutes. Carefully loosen loaves and invert pan onto shallow baking pan to remove loaves. Bake 20 minutes more. Combine remaining tomato sauce, brown sugar, and worcestershire. Heat and pass with meat. Serves 6.

Note: If you don't have the small fluted tube pans, use eight 6-ounce custard cups.

Mustard-Glazed Ham Loaf

 3 beaten eggs
 ½ cup tomato juice
 ½ cup finely crushed saltine crackers
    (14 crackers)
 2 tablespoons chopped onion
 1 tablespoon prepared horseradish
 ½ teaspoon salt
 ⅛ teaspoon pepper
 1½ pounds ground fully cooked ham
 1 pound ground pork
    Mustard Sauce

In bowl combine eggs and tomato juice; stir in cracker crumbs, onion, horseradish, salt, and pepper. Add ham and pork; mix well. In shallow baking dish shape meat mixture into a 9x5-inch loaf. Bake in 350° oven for 1¼ hours. Drain fat from ham loaf; pour Mustard Sauce over. Bake 30 minutes more, basting with sauce occasionally. Makes 8 to 10 servings.

Mustard Sauce: In bowl thoroughly combine ½ cup packed *brown sugar,* 2 tablespoons *vinegar,* and ½ teaspoon *dry mustard.*

Ham Bones and Pork Hocks

Spicy Hopping John

    8 cups water
    1 pound dry black-eyed peas (2⅔ cups)
    1 16-ounce can tomatoes, cut up
    1 cup chopped onion
    1 cup chopped celery
    1 tablespoon salt
    2 teaspoons chili powder
   ¼ teaspoon dried basil, crushed
    1 bay leaf
 1½ pounds smoked pork hocks
    1 cup long grain rice

In Dutch oven combine water and peas. Bring to boiling. Reduce heat; simmer 2 minutes. Remove from heat. Cover and let stand 1 hour. (Or, soak peas in water overnight.) *Do not drain.* Stir in *undrained* tomatoes, onion, celery, salt, chili powder, basil, and bay leaf. Add pork hocks. Cover; simmer about 1¼ hours. Remove pork hocks; cool slightly. Cut off meat; chop. Return meat to pea mixture; stir in rice. Cover; cook about 20 minutes or till rice is tender. Remove bay leaf. Add additional hot water and pass bottled hot pepper sauce, if desired. Serves 12.

Pork Hocks 'n Greens

    1 pound mustard greens
   ½ pound turnip greens
   ½ pound collard greens
    4 cups water
 3½ pounds smoked pork hocks
       Hard-cooked egg slices (optional)
       Corn Bread

Discard stems of greens and any damaged portions. Tear up large leaves. In Dutch oven combine water and pork hocks; bring to boiling. Add mustard, turnip, and collard greens; return to boiling. Reduce heat; cover and simmer for 1½ hours. About ½ hour before greens are done, prepare Corn Bread. To serve, ladle greens and juices (pot liquor) into bowl; garnish with hard-cooked egg slices, if desired. Serve pork hocks in another bowl. Pass Corn Bread. Serves 4.

Corn Bread: In mixing bowl stir together 1 cup all-purpose *flour,* 1 cup *yellow cornmeal,* ¼ cup *sugar,* 4 teaspoons *baking powder,* and ¾ teaspoon *salt.* Add 1 cup *milk,* 2 *eggs,* and ¼ cup *cooking oil.* Beat with rotary beater or electric mixer about 1 minute or just till smooth; do not overbeat. Bake in greased 9x9x2-inch baking pan in 350° oven for 20 to 25 minutes. Cut into squares.

Hot and Hearty Ham Soup

    8 cups water
    1 1½- to 1¾-pound meaty ham bone *or*
         1½ pounds smoked pork hocks
    8 whole black peppercorns
    5 whole cloves
    1 teaspoon salt
    1 clove garlic, minced
   ½ head cabbage, coarsely chopped
    2 large potatoes, peeled and thinly sliced
    3 large carrots, thinly sliced (2 cups)
    1 medium onion, chopped
    6 to 8 thick slices rye bread, toasted
   ¼ cup grated parmesan cheese
    4 ounces Swiss cheese, cut into strips

In 4½-quart Dutch oven combine water, ham bone or hocks, peppercorns, cloves, salt, and garlic. Bring to boiling; reduce heat. Cover and simmer 2½ hours. Remove ham bone or hocks; cool slightly. Cut off meat and chop. Strain broth; return broth and meat to Dutch oven. Add vegetables. Cover; simmer about 40 minutes or till vegetables are tender. Season to taste with salt and pepper. Ladle soup into heat-proof bowls. Top each with a slice of toast. Sprinkle with parmesan; top with strips of Swiss cheese. Place under broiler about 2 minutes or till cheese melts. (Or, if you don't have heat-proof bowls, place toast slices on baking sheet; top with cheeses and broil. Float atop soup servings.) Makes 6 to 8 servings.

Bean and Squash Soup

    1 pound dry navy beans (2⅓ cups)
    2 pounds winter squash, peeled, seeded, and cubed (about 4 cups)
    1 meaty ham bone (about 1 pound)
    1 cup chopped onion
    1 cup chopped celery

In 5-quart Dutch oven combine navy beans and 8 cups *water.* Bring to boiling; simmer 2 minutes. Remove from heat. Cover and let stand 1 hour. (Or, soak beans in water overnight.) *Do not drain.* Add *half* the winter squash, the ham bone, onion, celery, 1½ teaspoons *salt,* and ¼ teaspoon *pepper.* Bring to boiling. Reduce heat; cover and simmer 1½ hours. Remove ham bone; cool slightly. Partially mash beans. Cut meat from ham bone and chop. Return meat to Dutch oven along with remaining winter squash. Cover and simmer 20 minutes. Season to taste. Serves 8 to 10.

Chuck Wagon Bean Soup

 8 cups water
 1 pound dry pinto beans (2½ cups)
 1 16-ounce can tomatoes, cut up
 4 medium carrots, finely chopped (2 cups)
 1 cup chopped onion
 ¼ cup vinegar
 ¼ cup chili sauce
 2 tablespoons brown sugar
 2 tablespoons worcestershire sauce
 1 tablespoon salt
 2 teaspoons prepared mustard
 1 1-pound meaty ham bone *or* 2 smoked
     pork hocks

In Dutch oven combine water and beans. Bring to boiling; simmer 2 minutes. Remove from heat. Cover and let stand 1 hour. (Or, soak beans in water overnight.) *Do not drain.* Stir in vegetables, vinegar, chili sauce, sugar, worcestershire, salt, and mustard. Add ham bone or hocks. Bring to boiling. Cover; simmer 2½ to 3 hours or till beans are tender. Remove ham bone or hocks; cool slightly. Cut off meat and chop. Return meat to soup. Mash beans slightly, if desired. Serves 8 to 10.

Split Pea Soup

 1 pound dry green split peas (2¼ cups)
 8 cups water
 1 meaty ham bone (about 1½ pounds)
 1 cup chopped onion
 1 teaspoon instant chicken bouillon
     granules
 ½ teaspoon salt
 ¼ teaspoon pepper
 1 cup sliced carrot
 1 cup chopped celery
 2 slices bacon
 ½ cup light cream
 2 tablespoons butter *or* margarine

Rinse peas. In Dutch oven combine peas, water, ham bone, onion, bouillon granules, salt, and pepper. Bring to boiling. Reduce heat; cover and simmer 1½ hours, stirring often. Remove ham bone; cool slightly. Cut off meat and chop. Return meat to soup; add carrot and celery. Simmer 30 minutes. Cook bacon till crisp; drain and crumble. Stir bacon, light cream, and butter into soup; heat through. Makes 8 servings.

Pork Hocks and Black-Eyed Peas

12 cups water
 3 cups dry black-eyed peas (18 ounces)
 3 pounds smoked pork hocks
1½ cups chopped onion
 1 cup chopped celery
 1 bay leaf
 1 teaspoon salt
 ⅛ teaspoon cayenne
10 ounces okra, cut up (2 cups), *or* one
     10-ounce package frozen cut okra

In 6-quart Dutch oven combine water and peas. Bring to boiling; simmer 2 minutes. Remove from heat. Cover and let stand 1 hour. (Or, soak peas in water overnight.) *Do not drain.*

Add pork hocks, onion, celery, bay leaf, salt, and cayenne. Bring to boiling. Reduce heat; cover and simmer about 1½ hours or till pork hocks are tender and peas are done. Stir in fresh or frozen okra; cook 10 to 15 minutes or till okra is very tender. Remove bay leaf. Season to taste with salt and pepper. Serves 6.

Bean-Vegetable Soup

 1 pound dry navy beans (2⅓ cups)
 8 cups water
1½ pounds smoked pork hocks
 2 medium potatoes, peeled and cubed
     (2 cups)
 2 medium carrots, chopped (1 cup)
 2 stalks celery, sliced (1 cup)
 1 medium onion, chopped (½ cup)
 ¾ teaspoon dried thyme, crushed
 ½ teaspoon salt
 ¼ teaspoon pepper
     Several dashes bottled hot pepper
     sauce

Rinse beans. In 4-quart Dutch oven combine the water and beans. Bring to boiling; simmer 2 minutes. Remove from heat. Cover and let stand 1 hour. (Or, soak beans in water overnight in a covered pan.) *Do not drain.* Bring beans and liquid to boiling. Add pork hocks. Reduce heat; cover and simmer for 1 hour or till beans are nearly tender. Remove hocks; cool slightly. Cut off meat and coarsely chop. Discard bones. Return meat to pan. Add remaining ingredients. Cover and simmer 30 minutes or till vegetables are tender. Season to taste with salt and pepper. Serves 8 to 10.

Bacon

Bean-Bacon Chowder

- 6 slices bacon, cut up
- 1 cup chopped onion
- 2 tablespoons all-purpose flour
- 3 cups milk
- 2 medium potatoes, peeled and diced
- 1 teaspoon salt
- ¼ teaspoon dried thyme, crushed
- ⅛ teaspoon pepper
- 1 22-ounce jar baked beans
- ¼ cup snipped parsley

In saucepan cook bacon and onion till bacon is lightly browned and onion is tender. Blend in flour. Add milk; cook and stir till bubbly. Add potatoes, salt, thyme, and pepper. Cover; simmer 12 to 15 minutes or till potatoes are done. Stir in beans; heat through. Top with snipped parsley. Makes 6 servings.

Hearty Brunch Casserole

- 1 9-ounce package frozen French toast
- 6 slices Canadian-style bacon
- 6 hard-cooked eggs, sliced
- 1 11-ounce can condensed cheddar cheese soup
- ¼ cup milk
- 2 tablespoons chopped pimiento

Arrange frozen toast slices in a 12x7½x2-inch baking dish. Top with Canadian bacon slices and hard-cooked egg slices. Stir together soup, milk, and pimiento; spoon over eggs. Bake, covered, in 400° oven for 30 minutes. Uncover; bake about 10 minutes more. Makes 6 servings.

Cooking Bacon

Canadian-Style Bacon: Slice ¼ inch thick; slash edges. To broil, place on unheated rack in broiler pan. Broil 3 to 4 inches from heat 1 to 2 minutes per side. To pan-fry, cook slices in a little cooking oil 2 to 3 minutes per side.

Bacon: To cook in the oven, place bacon strips on unheated rack in shallow baking pan. Bake in 400° oven about 10 minutes. To broil, place bacon strips on unheated rack in broiler pan. Broil 3 to 5 inches from heat till desired doneness, turning once and watching closely.

Hot Potato Salad

- 4 large potatoes, peeled and cubed (6 cups)
- 1 cup thinly sliced carrot
- ½ cup chopped celery
- 8 slices bacon
- ¼ cup chopped onion
- 2 tablespoons all-purpose flour
- 2 tablespoons sugar
- ½ teaspoon salt
- ½ cup vinegar
- ½ cup mayonnaise or salad dressing
- 2 hard-cooked eggs, chopped
- 2 tablespoons snipped parsley

Cook potatoes, carrot, and celery in boiling water 12 to 15 minutes or till tender; drain. Cook bacon till crisp; drain, reserving 2 tablespoons drippings. Crumble bacon; set aside. Cook onion in reserved drippings till tender. Blend in flour, sugar, salt, and ⅛ teaspoon *pepper*. Stir in vinegar and ½ cup *water;* cook and stir till thickened and bubbly. Remove from heat; stir in mayonnaise, eggs, parsley, and crumbled bacon. Pour over vegetables; toss. Turn into 1½-quart casserole. Bake, covered, in 350° oven for 35 to 40 minutes or till heated through. Makes 6 to 8 servings.

Orange-Glazed Canadian Bacon

- 8 slices Canadian-style bacon, cut ½ inch thick
- 1 tablespoon butter or margarine
- ¼ cup pineapple preserves
- 3 tablespoons frozen orange juice concentrate, thawed
- 2 teaspoons lemon juice
- 1 teaspoon prepared mustard
- ⅛ teaspoon ground cloves

In a skillet lightly brown bacon, half at a time, on both sides in butter or margarine. Return all to skillet. For glaze, stir together remaining ingredients; pour over bacon. Bring just to boiling; reduce heat slightly and cook, uncovered, about 5 minutes or till of glaze consistency. Transfer bacon to platter; spoon glaze over meat. Serves 6 to 8.

Pineapple-Glazed Canadian Bacon: Prepare as above *except* substitute ¼ cup *orange marmalade* and 3 tablespoons frozen *pineapple juice concentrate,* thawed, for the pineapple preserves and orange juice concentrate.

Banana, water chestnut, and pineapple or kumquat are the surprise fillings in Appetizer Bacon Rolls.

Appetizer Bacon Rolls

    6 slices bacon, halved crosswise *or* 4
        slices Canadian-style bacon, cut ¼
        inch thick and each cut into thirds
    1 small firm banana, sliced 1 inch thick
    4 small canned water chestnuts
    4 pineapple chunks *or* preserved
        kumquats
1½ teaspoons cornstarch
    1 teaspoon dry mustard
    ⅛ teaspoon ground ginger
    ¼ cup currant jelly
    3 tablespoons frozen orange juice
        concentrate, thawed
    1 tablespoon lemon juice
        Dash bottled hot pepper sauce

Partially cook halved bacon slices. Roll each piece of meat around a banana piece, water chestnut, pineapple chunk, or kumquat. Secure with wooden picks. Place on rack in unheated broiler pan. For sauce, combine cornstarch, mustard, and ginger. Blend in remaining ingredients and ½ cup *water*. Cook and stir till thickened and bubbly. Brush bacon rolls with sauce. Broil 3 to 4 inches from heat for 3 to 4 minutes. Turn; brush with sauce. Broil 2 to 3 minutes more. Reheat remaining sauce; use for dipping. Makes 12.

Bacon-Leek Pie

    6 slices bacon, cut into 1-inch pieces
    6 medium leeks, thinly sliced (2 cups)
    1 tablespoon all-purpose flour
    1 teaspoon salt
    ½ teaspoon celery seed
    ¼ teaspoon pepper
1⅓ cups light cream
    3 tablespoons dry sherry
    5 slightly beaten eggs
    1 unbaked 9-inch pastry shell
        Ground nutmeg

Cook bacon till crisp. Drain; reserving ¼ cup drippings. Set bacon aside. Cook leeks in reserved drippings till tender but not brown, stirring occasionally. Blend in flour, salt, celery seed, and pepper. Add cream. Cook and stir till thickened and bubbly. Stir in sherry. Gradually stir hot mixture into beaten eggs. Stir in bacon. Pour into pastry shell; sprinkle lightly with nutmeg. Bake in 400° oven for 20 to 25 minutes or till knife inserted off-center comes out clean. Let stand 5 minutes. Serves 6.

Spaghetti with Canadian Bacon

    1 cup light cream
    2 tablespoons butter *or* margarine
    1 cup shredded mozzarella cheese
        (4 ounces)
    ½ cup ricotta *or* cream-style cottage cheese
    1 tablespoon all-purpose flour
    ⅛ teaspoon ground nutmeg
        White pepper
    ½ cup chopped onion
    1 clove garlic, minced
    1 tablespoon butter *or* margarine
    1 tablespoon olive *or* cooking oil
    1 cup chopped Canadian-style bacon
        (5 ounces)
    1 cup coarsely chopped fresh mushrooms
    ½ teaspoon dried marjoram, crushed
    2 tablespoons dry sherry
    8 ounces spaghetti, cooked, drained, and
        buttered

In blender container combine cream and 2 tablespoons butter or margarine; add mozzarella cheese, ricotta or cottage cheese, flour, and nutmeg. Cover; blend till smooth. Pour into 1½-quart saucepan. Cook and stir till mixture thickens and cheese melts. Season to taste with white pepper and salt. Keep cheese sauce warm but *do not boil*.

In skillet cook onion and garlic in 1 tablespoon butter or margarine and the oil till onion is tender but not brown. Stir in Canadian bacon, mushrooms, and marjoram. Cook 3 to 4 minutes, stirring occasionally. Stir in sherry; boil gently about 10 minutes or till liquid evaporates. Place hot spaghetti on large platter; top with warm cheese sauce. Spoon meat mixture over; toss. Makes 4 to 6 servings.

Buying Bacon

When buying bacon, remember to compare prices by cost per pound not cost per package. To compare the price of different size packages, divide the price of a 16-ounce package by 4; divide the price of a 12-ounce package by 3. The smaller the answer, the better the buy.

Sausage

Serve versatile sausages and discover their tangy, mild, sweet, and spicy flavors. Many popular and delightfully unusual sausages are described in the following pages. You'll find that from one sausage variety to another seasoning blends differ (often depending on an ethnic influence) from such exotic seasonings as pistachio nuts to simple ones such as garlic. Experiment with a variety of sausages to find your favorite flavor, texture, and shape. Be sure to check the next page for useful storage and cooking requirements for each type of sausage. Prepare quick snacks or easy meals with sausages that require little or no cooking. Throughout this chapter are taste-tempting recipes using frankfurters, or link, bulk, dry, and semi-dry sausages. Be adventuresome. Make home-made sausage links and vary the seasonings! Sausage—broiled, baked, grilled, steamed, stuffed, or skewered—adds full flavor and variety to your meals.

Sausage Identification

1	Genoa Salami	11	Bratwurst
2	Summer Sausage	12	Souse
3	Thuringer Cervelat	13	Beerwurst
4	Mettwurst	14	Blood and Tongue
5	Head Cheese	15	Cotto Salami
6	Blood Sausage	16	Prosciutto
7	Knackwurst	17	Mortadella
8	Liverwurst	18	Chorizo
9	Italian Sausage	19	Salami
10	Polish Sausage or Kielbasa	20	Beerwurst

Identifying Sausage

Sausages, because of the many variables in making them, come in a wide variety of flavors, shapes, and textures. A sausage may be pork, beef, veal, lamb, or a combination of these; but it is the unique blend of seasonings that gives a sausage its individuality. The sausage shape is determined by its casing, which is either natural (that is, of animal origin) or manufactured. Manufactured casings may be edible or non-edible. Sausage may be cured, smoked, dried, and/or cooked. All these variables determine the final, distinctive character of each sausage variety.

The kind and amount of processing that a sausage receives determines its storage and cooking requirements. Check the label to see whether cooking is needed. If the sausage is bought over the counter, ask the meat man whether it is uncooked or cooked. Use the following descriptions as a reference.

TYPES OF SAUSAGE

Fresh: Made from uncured, uncooked meat. Some may be smoked. This group includes pork sausage, fresh bratwurst, and fresh Polish sausage. Treat like fresh meat. Keep refrigerated. Use within 3 or 4 days of purchasing. Cook thoroughly. Allow 4 or 5 servings per pound.

Uncooked, smoked: Made from cured meat. Smoking adds flavor and color. This group includes mettwurst and linguisa. Keep refrigerated. Use within 1 week of purchasing. Most smoked sausages must be thoroughly cooked unless labeled "fully cooked," "ready-to-eat," or "do not cook." Allow 4 or 5 servings per pound.

Cooked: Made from fresh meats that may be either cured or uncured. This group includes blood sausage, cooked bratwurst, liver sausage, and yachtwurst. Keep refrigerated. Use within 1 week of purchasing. Ready to eat. Generally served cold. Allow 4 or 5 servings per pound.

Cooked, smoked: Made from fresh meats that are smoked and fully cooked. This group includes wieners, smoked sausage links, and knackwurst. Keep refrigerated. Use within 1 week of purchasing (2 weeks if unopened in original vacuum package). Ready to eat but usually served hot. Allow 4 or 5 servings per pound.

Dry, Semi-Dry: Made from cured meats that are either smoked or unsmoked. Cured and dried through a process of bacterial fermentation, which develops flavor and acts as a preservative. Allow 8 servings per pound.

Most *dry* sausages are salamis. The casings become shriveled and texture is very firm. Cool storage is recommended.

Semi-dry sausages are generally softer and include most cervelats. Keep refrigerated.

Prepared Meats: Cured meats are often thought of as sausages. This group includes cappicola and pastrami. May be smoked or unsmoked. Keep refrigerated. Use within 1 week of purchasing. Ready to eat; usually served cold. Allow 4 to 6 servings per pound.

Cooked Meat Specialties: Typically called luncheon meats. Finely ground or puréed meat with spices and seasonings. Federal government regulates percentage of non-meat ingredients, such as cereal or dried milk, that may be added. May be cured. Fully cooked or baked. Keep refrigerated. Allow 4 or 5 servings per pound. Includes such items as olive loaf, pickle and pimiento loaf, old-fashioned loaf, and honey loaf.

Beerwurst

Also called Beer Salami. Pork and beef; chopped. May be all pork. Seasoning includes garlic. Natural casings or bulk pieces for slicing. *(cooked, smoked)*

Berliner Sausage

Cured lean pork; coarsely ground. May include a small amount of beef or veal. Sugar and salt are the only seasonings. Packaged in slices or in bulk rolls for slicing. Variety known as Dutch Berliner has bacon, eggs, onion, and spices. *(cooked, smoked)*

Blood Sausage

Also called Blutwurst, Blood Pudding or Long Blood Sausage, Pepper Blood (links), Bloodwurst, or Biroldo. Pork fat cooked and diced; cooked meat, finely ground; and beef blood. Spices

How to Cook Sausage

Fresh and uncooked sausages need to be thoroughly cooked before eating. Fully cooked sausages can be heated through if you want to serve them warm; or they may be served cold.

Uncooked Patties: Place in an unheated skillet. Cook slowly, uncovered, for 15 to 20 minutes or till thoroughly cooked, turning once. Drain well. *Or,* arrange patties on unheated rack in a shallow baking pan. Bake in 400° oven for 20 to 25 minutes or till thoroughly cooked.

Uncooked Links: Do not prick. Place in an unheated skillet. Add ¼ cup cold *water* per half pound sausage. Cover and cook slowly for 5 minutes; drain well. Cook slowly, uncovered, 12 to 14 minutes more or till liquid from sausages has evaporated and sausages are thoroughly cooked, turning occasionally with tongs.

Fully Cooked Links: Add to boiling liquid (water, beer, or wine) in a saucepan. Reduce heat; cover and simmer for 5 to 10 minutes or till heated through.

include allspice, cloves, onion, salt, and pepper. May be smoked or unsmoked. Natural casings or bulk pieces for slicing. Other varieties include Black Pudding (English) with added cereal, Boudin Noir (French) with brandy, and Toscano (Italian) with raisins. *(cooked)*

Blood and Tongue Sausage

Pork and/or lamb tongues are cooked and cured, then placed in center of *Blood Sausage*. *(cooked)*

Bockwurst

Also called Swiss Sausages. May be veal and pork or all pork, plus milk, chives, eggs, and parsley. Seasonings similar to frankfurters. Generally available only from January to Easter. Popular at spring sausage festivals in Germany. Highly perishable. Light colored links about 5 inches long. *(fresh or cooked)*

Bologna

Beef and pork, finely ground and mildly seasoned. Also may be all beef, or pork, or ham. Typical seasonings include pepper, cloves, coriander, ginger, garlic, and nutmeg. Available in rings, chubs, and slices of varying diameters. Credited to Bologna, Italy. Many varieties, depending on spices and meats used. *(cooked, smoked)*

Bratwurst

All pork, or pork and beef, or pork and veal. Usually finely ground. Spice formulas vary. German meaning "frying sausage." Large links, often 1½ inches in diameter; usually 6 or 7 links per pound. *(fresh or cooked)*

Braunschweiger

Liver sausage that is smoked after cooking or includes smoked meats such as bacon. Also may

include milk and onions. Spices include coriander, ginger, marjoram, mustard, pepper, and salt. Smooth texture; may be sliced or spread. Credited to Brunswick, Germany. Available in various-size chubs and in whole pieces. Name also may be attached to other sausage types to indicate area of origin. *(cooked)* (See also *Liver Sausage.*)

Cappicola

Boneless pork shoulder seasoned with ground hot or sweet peppers, paprika, salt, and sugar. *(smoked; prepared meat)*

Cervelat

Often given the general name *Summer Sausage*. Beef and pork; usually finely ground. Garlic is generally not included in the seasonings. Many varieties differentiated by grind of meat, spices used, and degree of smoking. Sliced or in rolls. *(semi-dry)*

Chipolata

Also called Cipollata. Name sometimes used to mean very small sausages. Lean pork finely chopped, plus pork fat, coarsely chopped. May include rice and rusks plus salt, pepper, coriander, pimiento, nutmeg, and thyme. Links are usually 16 to 20 per pound. Italian; popular in France. *(fresh)*

Chorizo

Pork, coarsely chopped; seasoned with pimiento, sweet red pepper, and sometimes garlic. Looks similar to *Italian Pork Sausage*. Bulk and link forms. *(dry)*

Cooked Salami

Cured pork and beef, but definitely has a softer texture than dry and semi-dry salamis. Many varieties. *(cooked)*

Cotto Salami

Pork and beef, coarsely ground, or all beef. Mild flavor characterized by whole peppercorns.

May be smoked. Sliced and in rolls. *(cooked, smoked)*

Dried beef

Beef is cured, smoked, dehydrated, and thinly sliced. *(prepared meat)*

Farmer Cervelat

Also may be called Farmer Sausage, *Cervelat*, or Bauernwurst. Pork, coarsely chopped, and beef, finely chopped. Mild seasonings include mustard, pepper, salt, and sugar. Natural casings, usually about 2 inches in diameter. *(dry)*

Frankfurters

Pork and beef, ground, or all beef. Typical seasonings include coriander, garlic or onion, dry mustard, paprika, nutmeg, salt, sugar, pepper, cloves, and mace. Credited to Frankfurt, Germany. Originally used beef and pork, and had more seasonings (especially garlic) than wieners. Various sizes. May be skinless or have natural casings. *(cooked, smoked)* (See also *Wieners.*)

Fresh Polish Sausage

Pork shoulder, coarsely chopped. Seasonings include garlic, marjoram, salt, sugar, and pepper. Usually in 10- to 14-inch links. *(fresh)* (See also *Polish Sausage.*)

Fresh Thuringer

Pork or pork and veal; finely ground. May include dry milk solids, plus coriander, ginger, ground celery seed, mace, pepper, salt, and sugar. Usually in links, 3 to 5 per pound. *(fresh)* (See also *Smoked Thuringer.*)

Frizzes

Cured lean pork, sometimes with added cured lean beef; coarsely chopped. Some varieties made with hot spices; others with sweet spices. Irregularly shaped; natural casings. *(dry)*

Genoa Salami

May be called Italian or Hard Salami. Usually all pork, coarsely ground; may use some beef. Garlic and wine or grape juice added. Unsmoked. Firm texture with flavor sometimes compared to aged cheese. Natural casings; about 3-inch diameter. Credited to Genoa, Italy. Name may be attached to other sausages to indicate area of origin. *(dry)*

German Salami

Also called Hard Salami. Beef and pork in equal amounts; coarsely cut. Seasonings are salt, pepper, garlic, and sugar. May be lightly smoked. Sliced or chub; about 3½-inch diameter. *(dry)*

Goteborg Cervelat

Also called Swedish Sausage. Pork and beef, coarsely chopped. Heavily smoked. Sweet flavor from the spice, cardamom; also tends to be salty. Described as a hard cervelat. *(dry, semi-dry)*

Head Cheese

Chopped, cured pork head meat in gelatin base. Seasonings often include caraway, coriander, mustard, red pepper, salt, sage, and thyme. Colorful. *(cooked meat specialty)*

Holsteiner

Similar in flavor and texture to *Farmer Cervelat* but has larger diameter and is often ring shaped. *(dry)*

Italian Pork Sausage

Also called Salsiccia. Pork, coarsely or finely chopped. May include some beef. Seasoned with fennel, garlic, coriander, nutmeg, paprika, and sometimes red pepper. Bulk, sometimes links. *(fresh)*

Italian Salami

Usually cured lean pork; may have some beef. Seasonings often include garlic, cinnamon, cloves, nutmeg, salt, sugar, pepper, and peppercorns. May be moistened with red wine or grape juice. Never smoked. Includes many varieties. *(dry, semi-dry)*

Kielbasa

See *Polish Sausage.*

Knackwurst

Also called Knoblauch, Knochblauc, and Garlic Sausage. Beef and pork with coriander, garlic, nutmeg, salt, sugar, and pepper. Four-inch links usually served hot. *(cooked, smoked)*

Kosher Salami

Kosher beef, ground, plus cubes of fat. Seasonings include coriander, garlic, nutmeg, mustard, pepper, salt, and sugar. Meat and processing are under Rabbinical supervision. *(semi-dry)*

Krakow

Lean pork, coarsely ground, and beef, finely chopped. Seasoned with pepper, garlic, salt, and sugar. Usually has 3-inch diameter. Polish and German. Similar to *New England-Brand Sausage.* *(cooked, smoked)*

Landjaeger Cervelat

Beef and pork, or all beef with mustard, pepper, caraway, salt, and sugar. Heavily smoked and dried giving a black, wrinkled appearance. Links are pressed to give flattened shape. Swiss. *(dry)*

Lebanon Bologna

Lean beef, coarsely chopped. Seasoned with cloves, coriander, garlic, ginger, pepper, salt, and sugar. Heavily smoked. Tangy flavor. Dark surface appearance. Sliced or in rolls. Credited to Pennsylvania Dutch in Lebanon, Pennsylvania. *(semi-dry)*

Linguisa

Also called Longanzia. Pork, coarsely ground with garlic, cumin seed, and cinnamon. Cured in brine before stuffing. Portuguese. *(uncooked, smoked)*

Liver Cheese

Also called Liver Loaf. Similar to *Liver Sausage* but with firmer texture. May be seasoned with coriander, ginger, mustard, onion, and pepper. Usually wrapped in white pork fat. Square shape, about 4 inches. *(cooked)*

Liver Sausage

Also called Liverwurst. Pork jowls and liver, finely ground. Smooth texture; slices or spreads easily. Seasonings include cloves, mace, marjoram, onion, salt, sugar, and pepper. Ring shaped or in roll. One variety combines goose livers, diced pork tongues, and pistachio nuts. *(cooked)*

Mettwurst

Also called Teawurst or Smearwurst. Cured beef and pork, finely chopped. Seasoned with allspice, coriander, ginger, mustard, salt, pepper, and sugar. Spreading consistency. German. Name also may be given to a semi-dry, coarsely ground sausage. *(uncooked, smoked)*

Mortadella

Pork, finely chopped, plus cubed pork fat. May add beef. Seasoned with anise, coriander, garlic, and peppercorns. Italian. Natural casing. *(dry)*

Mortadella, German-Style

Lean cuts of pork and beef, finely ground, plus diced pork fat and pistachio nuts. Seasoned similar to a large bologna. Natural casing. *(cooked, smoked)*

New England Sausage

Cured lean pork, coarsely chopped. May have cloves. Ham-like flavor. Large diameter rolls. Must be labeled New England-style or brand when made outside New England. *(cooked, smoked)*

Pastrami

Flat pieces of lean beef are cured, then rubbed with spices including garlic and cumin. *(smoked; prepared meat)*

Pepperoni

Beef and pork, coarsely chopped. Highly seasoned with red pepper and paprika. Available in chubs, sliced, and in paired links, 10 to 12 inches long and about 1½ inches in diameter. *(dry)*

Polish Sausage

Also called Kielbasa, Kolbassy, or Kobasa. Pork, coarsely chopped, and beef, finely chopped. Seasoned with coriander, garlic, marjoram, salt, pepper, and sugar. May be uncooked. Links, 6 to 14 inches long; longer ones may be tied in ring shape. *(cooked, smoked)* (See also *Fresh Polish Sausage.*)

Pork Sausage

Ground pork seasoned with pepper, nutmeg, and sage. Sold in bulk, patties, or links. Country-style variety is coarsely ground, mildly cured, and may be smoked or unsmoked. *(fresh)*

Potato Sausage

Beef and pork, finely chopped; mixed with potatoes. Seasonings include ginger, mace, onion, sage, salt, sugar, and pepper. *(fresh)*

Prosciutto

Ham that is dry-cured under pressure. Spices rubbed in to ensure even distribution of flavor. Has no casing. Slice thinly. *(prepared meat)*

Salami

Sometimes called Dry or Hard Salami to differentiate from Cooked Salami which is more perishable. This is a general category of highly seasoned sausages having a characteristic fermented flavor. Pork and beef with added garlic, pepper, salt, and sugar. May or may not be smoked. *(dry)* (See also *Cooked Salami, Cotto Salami, Genoa Salami, German Salami, Italian Salami,* and *Kosher Salami.*)

Scrapple

Ground cooked pork trimmings such as heart, liver, and tongue, plus cornmeal. Other flours may be added in small amounts. Seasonings include pepper, sage, and salt. Available in rolls or canned. To serve, slice and fry. Pennsylvania Dutch specialty. *(cooked meat specialty)*

Smoked Sausage Links

Beef and pork or all pork, coarsely ground. Seasoned with pepper; smoked. Size of links varies. Developed in Wisconsin in late 1940s. *(cooked, smoked)*

Smoked Thuringer Links

Beef and pork, coarsely chopped. Seasonings include mustard, garlic, salt, sugar, and pepper. Usually 5 or 6 links per pound. *(cooked, smoked)* (See also *Fresh Thuringer.*)

Souse

Also called Sulze or Sylta. Ground pork. Similar to *Head Cheese* but with a more sweet-sour flavor from addition of vinegar, pickles, and pimiento. *(cooked meat specialty)*

Summer Sausage

Properly used to describe all dry sausage, but especially refers to mildly seasoned soft cervelats such as *Thuringer Cervelat.* Originally made during the winter for summer use. Air drying removes much moisture giving them good keeping qualities. Typical lactic acid tartness. *(semi-dry, dry)*

Thuringer Cervelat

Beef and pork combination, or beef or pork alone. Mildly seasoned with coriander, pepper, cardamom, ginger, and mustard. Usually smoked. Often described as having the most-tangy, fermented flavor of all cervelats. Credited to Province of Thuringia, Germany. Usually in rolls with about 2½-inch diameter. Name may be attached to other sausage varieties to indicate area of origin. *(semi-dry)* (See also *Fresh* and *Smoked Thuringer.*)

Weisswurst

Pork and veal. Seasonings include mace, parsley, sage, thyme, lemon peel, salt, and sugar. Light color and delicate flavor. German, meaning "white sausage." Plump links about 4 inches long. Similar to cooked bratwurst. *(fresh)*

Wieners

Beef, pork, and sometimes veal, finely chopped. Ratio of the meats used varies with market price; most-used ingredient must be listed first on the label. Seasonings may include allspice, coriander, sugar, ginger, salt, and pepper. Credited to Vienna, Austria. *(cooked, smoked)* (See also *Frankfurters.*)

Yachtwurst

Lean pork, coarsely chopped. May add beef. Includes pistachio nuts and garlic. *(cooked)*

Create a Deli Tray

For either a light meal or a sausage-tasting party, create a deli tray. By making it yourself, it will be less expensive than a store-bought one, and you decide which foods to serve your guests. Choose a variety of sausages, cheeses, and breads, and add complementing condiments. Count on 6 to 8 servings per pound of sausage or cheese.

Sausage: Serve several types of sausage so everyone can taste a sample of different varieties. Some sausages to include are berliner sausage, blood sausage, blood and tongue sausage, Lebanon bologna, braunschweiger, cervelat, cotto salami, Genoa salami, liver cheese, liver sausage, and mortadella.

Cheese: Complement the flavor of sausage by serving it with cheeses such as brick, monterey jack, muenster, blarney, sharp cheddar, Swiss, colby, caraway, edam, and gouda.

Breads: Favorite breads to serve include whole wheat, sourdough, dark rye, bagels, pumpernickel, and individual French rolls.

Present an attractive deli tray by rolling or folding sausage and cheese slices, and arranging on a lettuce-lined platter or wooden tray. Alternate rows of meat and cheese by color, texture, and shape. In the center of the platter, place a pot of spicy mustard or mayonnaise. Garnish the arrangement with parsley sprigs, hard-cooked egg wedges, olives, cherry tomatoes, and radish roses.

The deli tray can be made several hours before serving time. Cover tightly with clear plastic wrap to prevent the food from drying out and refrigerate. If you plan to serve a large group, prepare two or more deli trays. Serve one and keep back-ups fresh in the refrigerator.

At serving time, have on hand plenty of sandwich-makings, such as tomato slices, lettuce, pickles, onion slices, relishes, horseradish, and butter or margarine. Besides the deli tray serve fresh fruits and vegetables or a tossed salad.

Make Your Own Sausage

A food grinder or a food processor is required for making sausage at home. After grinding and seasoning the meats, stuff them into casings. Use a hand stuffer or a stuffing attachment that fits another appliance. Cook and enjoy!

>   **Pork *or* beef sausage casings (12 to 15 feet)**
> 5 **pounds untrimmed boneless pork shoulder, cut into 1½-inch cubes (for Brats use 3 pounds boneless pork shoulder and 2 pounds boneless beef chuck)**
> 12 **ounces pork fat**
> 2 **cups water**
> 5 **teaspoons salt**
>   **Country-Style, Spicy Italian, *or* Brats Seasoning**

Run water through casings; soak in water at least 2 hours or overnight in refrigerator. With coarse blade of food grinder, grind pork and 12 ounces pork fat together. Add the 2 cups water, the salt, and desired seasoning mixture. Grind again. Attach sausage stuffer attachment to mixer or grinder. Using a 3- to 4-foot piece of casing at a time, push casing onto stuffer, letting some extend beyond end of attachment. Using coarse blade of grinder, grind mixture together, allowing it to fill casing. Fill casing till firm but not overly full, tying with string or twisting casing when links are 4 to 5 inches long. Wrap and chill immediately. Makes 5 pounds.

To cook sausages: Do not prick. Place in unheated skillet; add ½ cup cold *water* per half pound sausage. Cover and cook slowly for 5 minutes; drain. Cook slowly, uncovered, for 12 to 14 minutes, turning with tongs.

Country-Style Seasoning: Combine 2 tablespoons ground *sage;* 1 tablespoon dried *savory,* crushed; 1½ teaspoons *pepper;* 1½ teaspoons *cayenne;* and 1 teaspoon ground *nutmeg.* Add to meat mixture as directed.

Spicy Italian Seasoning: Combine 8 *bay leaves,* finely crushed; 5 cloves *garlic,* minced; 2 tablespoons *paprika;* 5 teaspoons dried *thyme,* crushed; 4 dried red *peppers,* crushed; 2 teaspoons *fennel seed,* crushed; 1 teaspoon *pepper;* and 1 teaspoon *cayenne.* Add to meat mixture as directed.

Brats Seasoning: Combine 4 teaspoons *sugar;* 4 teaspoons dried *rosemary,* crushed; 1 tablespoon ground *coriander;* 1 tablespoon *dry mustard;* 1 tablespoon ground *sage;* 1¼ teaspoons *pepper;* 1 teaspoon *paprika;* 1 teaspoon ground *nutmeg;* and ¾ teaspoon *cayenne.* Add to meat mixture as directed.

Frankfurters and Link Sausages

Golden-Sauced Franks

1 8-ounce can pineapple chunks (juice pack)
1 17-ounce can sweet potatoes (syrup pack), cut up
1 pound frankfurters, cut into 1-inch pieces
3 tablespoons brown sugar
1 tablespoon cornstarch
½ teaspoon finely shredded orange peel
¼ cup orange juice
1 tablespoon vinegar
1 tablespoon chili sauce

Drain pineapple, reserving juice. In 2-quart casserole combine pineapple, sweet potatoes, and franks. In small saucepan combine brown sugar and cornstarch. Stir in reserved pineapple juice, orange peel, orange juice, vinegar, chili sauce, and 2 tablespoons *water*. Cook and stir over medium heat till thickened and bubbly. Pour over mixture in casserole. Do not stir. Cover and bake in 350° oven for about 45 minutes or till heated through. Makes 4 to 6 servings.

Microwave directions: Drain pineapple, reserving juice. In 2-quart non-metal casserole combine pineapple, sweet potatoes, and franks. In a 2-cup glass measure combine the brown sugar and cornstarch. Stir in the reserved pineapple juice, remaining ingredients, and 2 tablespoons *water*. Cook, uncovered, in countertop microwave oven on high power about 2 minutes or till thickened and bubbly; stir after each minute. Pour sauce over mixture in casserole. Do not stir. Micro-cook, covered, for 9 to 10 minutes, stirring only once after 5 minutes.

Stuffed Baked Franks

1 pound large frankfurters (4 to 6)
¼ cup finely chopped onion
1 tablespoon butter *or* margarine
¼ cup catsup
2 cups herb-seasoned stuffing mix
⅓ cup shredded American cheese

Cut frankfurters lengthwise almost through to opposite side; place on baking sheet. Cook onion in butter till tender but not brown. In bowl combine onion, catsup, and ½ cup *water;* toss lightly with stuffing mix. Mound stuffing atop franks. Bake, covered, in 400° oven for about 10 minutes. Uncover. Sprinkle cheese atop each; bake 2 minutes more or till cheese melts. Makes 4 to 6 servings.

Quick Frank-Chili Soup

4 frankfurters, sliced
½ cup chopped onion
¼ cup chopped green pepper
3 tablespoons butter *or* margarine
1 8-ounce can pork and beans in tomato sauce
1 7½-ounce can tomatoes, cut up
1 to 1½ teaspoons chili powder

In saucepan cook frankfurters, onion, and green pepper in butter till onion is tender but not brown. Stir in remaining ingredients, ¼ cup *water,* and ⅛ teaspoon *salt.* Bring to boiling. Cover; simmer 5 to 10 minutes. Serves 3 or 4.

Coney Islands

½ pound ground beef
½ cup chopped onion
¼ cup chopped green pepper
1 8-ounce can tomato sauce
½ teaspoon chili powder
½ teaspoon paprika
⅛ teaspoon cayenne (optional)
1 pound frankfurters (8 to 10)
8 to 10 warm frankfurter buns

In skillet cook ground beef, onion, and green pepper till meat is browned. Drain. Add tomato sauce, chili powder, paprika, cayenne, ½ cup *water,* and ¼ teaspoon *salt.* Simmer 15 minutes. In saucepan cover frankfurters with cold water; bring to boiling. Simmer 5 minutes. To serve, place franks in buns and top each with a scant ¼ cup sauce. Makes 10 servings.

Tamale-Franks

1 15-ounce can tamales
1 pound frankfurters, cut up
1 11¼-ounce can condensed chili beef soup
1 8-ounce can tomato sauce
½ cup shredded cheddar cheese

Drain tamales, reserving sauce. Remove paper from tamales and cut each tamale into thirds. In 1½-quart casserole combine the reserved tamale sauce, frankfurters, soup, and tomato sauce. Top with tamales. Cover; bake in 350° oven for 35 minutes. Top with cheese and bake, uncovered, 10 minutes more. Serve with corn chips, if desired. Makes 6 servings.

Corn Dogs

    1 cup all-purpose flour
    ⅔ cup yellow cornmeal
    2 tablespoons sugar
    1½ teaspoons baking powder
    1 teaspoon salt
    ½ teaspoon dry mustard
    2 tablespoons shortening
    1 beaten egg
    ¾ cup milk
    1 pound frankfurters (8 to 10)
      Cooking oil

In bowl combine flour, cornmeal, sugar, baking powder, salt, and dry mustard. Cut in shortening till mixture resembles fine crumbs. Mix egg and milk. Add to dry ingredients; mix well. Insert wooden skewers in end of frankfurters. Pour oil into skillet to depth of 1 inch; heat to 375°. Coat franks with batter. (If batter is too thick, add 1 to 2 tablespoons *milk*.) Arrange coated franks 3 at a time in hot oil; turn franks with tongs after 10 seconds to prevent batter from sliding off. Cook 3 minutes, turning again halfway through cooking time. Serve hot with catsup and mustard, if desired. Makes 4 or 5 servings.

Sausage and Kraut

    4 slices bacon, cut into 1-inch pieces
    ½ pound boneless pork, cut into ½-inch
      cubes
    1 small onion, chopped (¼ cup)
    ½ pound Polish sausage, sliced
    2½ cups water
    ¼ cup dry white wine
    1 4-ounce can sliced mushrooms
    1½ teaspoons instant beef bouillon
      granules
    ¾ teaspoon paprika
    1 bay leaf
    1 16-ounce can sauerkraut, drained and
      snipped
    2 tablespoons cornstarch

In 3-quart saucepan cook bacon till crisp; drain bacon, reserving drippings. Set bacon aside. Brown pork cubes and onion in reserved drippings. Stir in bacon, sausage, water, wine, *un-drained* mushrooms, bouillon granules, paprika, and bay leaf. Cover; simmer about 1 hour or till meat is tender. Remove bay leaf. Stir in sauerkraut. Blend ¼ cup cold *water* into cornstarch. Add to sauerkraut mixture; cook and stir till thickened and bubbly. Makes 4 to 6 servings.

Kielbasa Pasta Salad

You can substitute potato sausage, weisswurst, or fresh bratwurst for the Polish sausage –

    12 ounces Polish sausage (Kielbasa)
    1½ cups large (1-inch) shell macaroni
    6 slices bacon
    1 cup sliced fresh mushrooms
    3 tablespoons sugar
    2 tablespoons all-purpose flour
    ½ teaspoon salt
    ¾ cup water
    ¼ cup tarragon vinegar
    2 tablespoons snipped parsley

In skillet simmer sausage, covered, in ½ cup *water* for 20 minutes. Meanwhile, cook macaroni according to package directions; drain. Drain and slice sausage; set aside. In large skillet cook bacon till crisp; drain, reserving 3 tablespoons drippings in skillet. Crumble bacon; set aside. Cook mushrooms in reserved drippings for 2 minutes. Stir in sugar, flour, salt, and ⅛ teaspoon *pepper;* add the ¾ cup water and the vinegar. Cook and stir till thickened and bubbly. Add sausage, macaroni, bacon, and parsley. Toss together lightly. Garnish with additional snipped parsley, if desired. Serves 4 to 6.

Polish Sausage Stew

    1 27-ounce can sauerkraut, drained
    1 10¾-ounce can condensed cream of
      celery soup
    1 soup can water (1¼ cups)
    ⅓ cup packed brown sugar
    1½ pounds Polish sausage, cut into 2-inch
      pieces
    4 medium potatoes, peeled and cubed
    1 cup chopped onion
    1 cup shredded monterey jack cheese

In Dutch oven combine sauerkraut, soup, water, and brown sugar. Stir in sausage, potatoes, and onion. Cover and simmer about 45 minutes or till potatoes are tender. Spoon off fat. Stir in shredded cheese. Spoon into serving bowls. Pass additional shredded monterey jack cheese to sprinkle atop, if desired. Serves 6 to 8.

Crockery cooker directions: In electric slow crockery cooker combine all ingredients *except* omit the 1¼ cups water and reserve the cheese. Cover and cook on low-heat setting for 8 hours. (Or, cook on high heat setting for 4 hours.) Spoon off excess fat. Stir in the 1 cup shredded cheese. Serve as above.

Polish Sausage Sandwich Bundle

1½ to 1¾ cups all-purpose flour
1 package active dry yeast
2 teaspoons caraway seed
1 cup warm water (110° to 115°)
¼ cup packed brown sugar
1½ teaspoons cooking oil
½ teaspoon salt
1¼ cups rye flour
½ cup mayonnaise *or* salad dressing
2 tablespoons chopped green pepper
2 tablespoons chopped pimiento
1 tablespoon sliced green onion
1 tablespoon chili sauce
6 Polish sausages
1 8-ounce can sauerkraut, drained and snipped
½ cup shredded Swiss *or* American cheese (2 ounces)
Milk

Combine 1¼ *cups* of the all-purpose flour, the yeast, and caraway seed. Blend together water, brown sugar, oil, and salt. Add to flour mixture. Beat at low speed of electric mixer for ½ minute, scraping bowl. Beat 3 minutes at high speed. Stir in rye flour and as much of the remaining ½ cup all-purpose flour as you can mix in using a spoon. Turn out onto a floured surface. Knead in enough of the remaining all-purpose flour to make a moderately stiff dough. Knead till smooth (about 5 minutes); dough will be sticky. Place in greased bowl; turn once.

Cover; let rise till double (about 1 hour). Punch down; turn out onto a lightly floured surface. Divide dough and shape into 6 balls. Cover; let rest 5 to 10 minutes.

Meanwhile, combine mayonnaise or salad dressing, green pepper, pimiento, sliced green onion, and chili sauce; mix well. Set aside.

To make sandwich bundles, place each ball of dough on a lightly floured surface. Roll to a rectangle 6 inches wide and 2 inches longer than each sausage, rolling thinner at edges. Place a Polish sausage in center of each rectangle, top with some of the sauerkraut, some mayonnaise mixture, and some shredded cheese. Fold two opposite edges of dough so they overlap atop filling. Fold remaining edges toward center to form a rectangular packet. Place seam down on ungreased baking sheet. Cover; let rise about 30 minutes. Brush tops with milk. Bake in a 425° oven about 10 minutes or till golden brown. Makes 6 sandwiches.

Lentils Coriander

1 pound Italian sausage links, cut into 1-inch pieces
2 large onions, thinly sliced
2 teaspoons ground coriander
1½ teaspoons salt
½ teaspoon ground ginger
2 cups dry lentils
1 tablespoon lemon juice
Dairy sour cream
Lemon slices

In Dutch oven brown sausage; stir in onions. Cover; cook till onion is tender but not brown. Drain off excess fat. Stir in coriander, salt, and ginger. Add lentils and 7 cups *water*. Bring to boiling. Reduce heat; cover and simmer for 50 minutes. Stir in lemon juice. Serve in soup bowls; top with a dollop of sour cream and a lemon slice. Makes 8 servings.

Italian Sausage Kabobs

Choose either mild or spicy Italian sausage links to suit your family's taste. Chipolata is a mild, flavorful Italian sausage you might try –

¼ cup finely chopped onion
2 tablespoons butter *or* margarine
½ cup apple cider *or* juice
¼ cup red wine vinegar
2 tablespoons honey
1 tablespoon bottled steak sauce
1 teaspoon salt
⅛ teaspoon pepper
2 pounds Italian sausage links
16 small onions (1 pound)
16 large mushroom caps
8 cherry tomatoes

For sauce, in small saucepan cook chopped onion in butter or margarine till tender but not brown. Stir in cider, vinegar, honey, steak sauce, salt, and pepper. Bring to boiling; simmer, uncovered, for 20 minutes, stirring occasionally.

Meanwhile, in large saucepan add sausage to boiling water. Reduce heat; cover and simmer for 10 minutes; drain. Cut crosswise into 2-inch pieces. Cook whole onions, uncovered, in boiling water for 3 to 5 minutes or till nearly tender; drain. On eight 10-inch skewers alternately thread sausage pieces, whole onions, and mushrooms. Grill over *hot* coals for 10 to 12 minutes, turning and brushing often with sauce. Garnish ends of skewers with cherry tomatoes. Heat and pass remaining sauce. Serves 8.

For a hearty meal, prepare Choucroute Garni, which means "sauerkraut with all the trimmings."

Choucroute Garni

1 medium onion, sliced
1 tablespoon bacon drippings *or* lard
3 fresh pork hocks (1½ pounds) *or*
   2 pounds pork spareribs, cut into
   3-rib portions
1 2-pound smoked pork shoulder roll *or*
   3 or 4 smoked pork loin rib chops,
   cut ¾ inch thick (1½ pounds)
3 16-ounce cans sauerkraut, rinsed and
   drained
2 cooking apples, peeled, cored, and cut
   into wedges
2 tablespoons brown sugar
4 whole cloves
3 juniper berries, crushed (optional)
2 small cloves garlic, minced
1 bay leaf
⅛ teaspoon freshly ground black pepper
1½ cups rhine wine
1 pound sausage links (use desired
   combination of fresh bratwurst, fresh
   bockwurst, fresh thuringer, precooked
   knackwurst, *and/or* precooked
   frankfurters
   Boiled potatoes

In 4½- or 5-quart Dutch oven cook onion in bacon drippings or lard about 5 minutes or till tender; remove from heat. Add pork hocks or spareribs. Cut pork shoulder roll crosswise into ¾-inch slices; add shoulder slices or loin chops to Dutch oven. In large bowl stir together the sauerkraut, apples, brown sugar, cloves, juniper berries, garlic, bay leaf, and pepper. Spoon over meats. Pour wine over all. Cover and bake in 375° oven 2½ hours or till meats are tender.

Meanwhile, prepare desired combination of sausages. For fresh bratwurst, bockwurst, and thuringer, place in unheated skillet with 2 to 3 tablespoons *water;* cover and cook over low heat 5 to 8 minutes. Uncover; cook 5 to 8 minutes more or till water has evaporated and sausages are cooked through. For knackwurst and frankfurters, add to boiling water in saucepan; cover and simmer 5 to 10 minutes or till heated through.

Mound sauerkraut mixture on deep, wide serving platter. Arrange meats and sausages around and atop sauerkraut. Add boiled potatoes to platter or pass separately. Makes 6 servings.

Note: Bratwurst, bockwurst, and thuringer links are also available precooked. These precooked types may be heated in boiling water as directed for knackwurst and frankfurters.

Bratwurst in Beer

1 pound bratwurst
½ cup chopped onion
2 tablespoons cooking oil
1 cup beer
1 cup beef broth
1 tablespoon brown sugar
2 bay leaves
¼ teaspoon pepper
¼ teaspoon dried thyme, crushed
¼ cup cold water
2 tablespoons all-purpose flour

In 10-inch skillet cook bratwurst and onion in oil over medium-low heat till bratwurst is brown and onion is tender. Drain off excess fat. Add beer, beef broth, brown sugar, bay leaves, pepper, and thyme. Simmer, uncovered, about 20 minutes or till done. Remove bratwurst and keep warm. Discard bay leaves. For sauce, blend water into flour; stir into hot beer mixture. Cook and stir till thickened and bubbly; pour over bratwurst and hot, cooked *noodles*. Serves 4.

Bratwurst Crepes

Process Swiss cheese will keep the sauce smooth and creamy –

1 12-ounce package fully cooked
   bratwurst, cut in half lengthwise
12 Crepes (see recipe, page 59)
2 tablespoons butter *or* margarine
2 tablespoons all-purpose flour
¾ teaspoon salt
¼ teaspoon ground nutmeg
   Dash pepper
1 cup light cream
¼ cup dry white wine
½ cup shredded Swiss cheese
1 3-ounce can sliced mushrooms, drained
   Snipped parsley (optional)

Place one bratwurst half on the unbrowned side of each crepe. Fold crepes so opposite edges overlap atop sausage. Place rolled crepes, seam side down, in a 13x9x2-inch baking dish. Cover with foil. Bake in 375° oven for 20 minutes or till heated through.

Melt butter or margarine in saucepan. Stir in flour, salt, nutmeg, and pepper. Add cream. Cook and stir till thickened and bubbly. Stir in wine; add cheese. Stir to melt cheese. Stir in mushrooms. Place two crepes on each plate. Spoon sauce atop crepes. Sprinkle with snipped parsley, if desired. Makes 6 servings.

Swiss Bratwurst Sandwich

Knackwurst is a tasty substitute for the bratwurst –

2 tablespoons butter *or* margarine
4 teaspoons all-purpose flour
¼ teaspoon salt
¼ teaspoon dry mustard
¾ cup milk
¾ cup shredded process Swiss cheese
    (3 ounces)
1 8-ounce can sauerkraut
4 cooked bratwurst
4 large slices pumpernickel bread, toasted
4 slices tomato
    Green pepper rings

Melt butter or margarine in small saucepan. Stir in flour, salt, and dry mustard; add milk. Cook and stir till thickened and bubbly. Stir in cheese till melted; cover and keep warm. Heat sauerkraut in small saucepan. Meanwhile, halve bratwurst lengthwise; place, cut side down, on broiler pan or baking sheet. Broil 3 to 5 inches from heat for 3 minutes.

Drain sauerkraut. For each sandwich, place 2 bratwurst halves on a bread slice. Top with ¼ of the hot sauerkraut and *1* of the tomato slices; spoon ¼ of the cheese sauce over. Garnish with a green pepper ring and sprinkle with a dash of ground nutmeg, if desired. Serves 4.

Puffed Potatoes and Sausage

¼ cup chopped green onion
2 tablespoons butter *or* margarine
3 medium potatoes, peeled and cubed
1 cup shredded American cheese
    (4 ounces)
⅓ cup milk
3 egg yolks
3 stiff-beaten egg whites
1 8-ounce package brown-and-serve
    sausage links

Cook green onion in butter or margarine till tender. Cook potatoes in boiling salted water about 10 minutes or till tender. Drain and mash (should measure 2 cups mashed potatoes). Beat in green onion and cheese. Beat together milk, egg yolks, and ½ teaspoon *salt;* add to potato mixture. Fold in egg whites. Turn into ungreased 2-quart casserole. Arrange sausage links atop. Bake in 375° oven 45 minutes. Makes 4 or 5 servings.

Liver and Sausage Supper

½ pound pork sausage links, cut into
    1-inch pieces
½ pound pork *or* beef liver, cut into strips
1 small onion, sliced
1 1-ounce envelope brown gravy mix
1½ cups water
1 8½-ounce can mixed vegetables,
    drained

In 10-inch skillet cook sausage over medium heat for 8 to 10 minutes or till browned. Drain, reserving 1 tablespoon drippings in skillet. Push sausage pieces to one side. Add liver and onion; cook over medium-high heat about 4 minutes or just till liver is done. Sprinkle gravy mix over all; stir to blend. Add water. Cook and stir till mixture is thickened and bubbly; stir in drained mixed vegetables and heat through. Serve meat-vegetable mixture over hot, cooked *rice.* Makes 4 servings.

Barbecued Beans and Smoked Sausage

1 16-ounce can pork and beans in tomato
    sauce
1 8¾-ounce can whole kernel corn, drained
1 7½-ounce can tomatoes, cut up
1 tablespoon brown sugar
1 tablespoon light molasses
2 teaspoons prepared mustard
1 12-ounce package fully cooked smoked
    sausage links, cut into thirds
½ cup shredded American cheese

In medium saucepan combine pork and beans, drained corn, *undrained* tomatoes, brown sugar, molasses and prepared mustard. Heat till boiling. Remove from heat; stir in sausage pieces. Turn mixture into 1½-quart casserole. Bake, uncovered, in a 350° oven for about 70 minutes, stirring twice during cooking time. Sprinkle cheese atop. Bake 2 to 3 minutes more or till cheese is melted. Makes 6 servings.

Bulk Sausage

Wine Spaghetti Sauce

1½ pounds bulk sweet Italian sausage *or*
    bulk pork sausage
1 cup chopped onion
¾ cup chopped green pepper
2 10¾-ounce cans condensed tomato
    soup
1 16-ounce can tomatoes, cut up
1 8-ounce can tomato sauce
1 cup dry red wine
2 bay leaves
1 teaspoon sugar
1 teaspoon dried oregano, crushed
1 teaspoon dried basil, crushed
2 4-ounce cans mushroom stems and
    pieces, drained

In Dutch oven cook sausage, onion, and green pepper till meat is browned; stir occasionally to break up sausage. Drain off fat. Stir in next 8 ingredients. Bring to boiling. Reduce heat; cook, uncovered, about 45 minutes or till desired consistency. Stir in mushrooms; heat through. Serve over hot, cooked *spaghetti*. Serves 8.

Crockery cooking direction: In skillet brown sausage; drain off fat. Transfer to an electric slow crockery cooker. Stir in remaining ingredients. Cover; cook on low-heat setting for 10 to 12 hours. Blend 2 tablespoons cold *water* into 2 tablespoons *cornstarch;* stir into sauce. Cook, covered, on high-heat setting for 10 minutes more. Serve as above.

Sausage-Apple Stuffed Squash

2 acorn squash, halved
¾ pound bulk pork sausage
¾ cup chopped celery
3 tablespoons chopped onion
1 medium cooking apple, peeled, cored,
    and chopped (1 cup)
1 slightly beaten egg
½ cup dairy sour cream
¾ cup shredded American cheese

Place squash halves, cut side down, in baking pan. Bake in 350° oven about 45 minutes or till tender. Sprinkle cut side with *salt*. In skillet cook sausage, celery, and onion till meat is browned. Stir in apple; cook 3 minutes more. Drain off fat. Combine egg and sour cream; stir into sausage mixture. Fill squash halves with sausage mixture. Bake 20 minutes. Sprinkle cheese atop. Bake 5 minutes more. Serves 4.

Easy Cassoulet

½ pound bulk pork sausage
1 small onion, sliced (½ cup)
1 clove garlic, minced
2 15-ounce cans navy beans
1½ cups cubed fully cooked ham
¼ cup dry white wine
2 tablespoons snipped parsley
1 bay leaf
    Dash ground cloves

In skillet cook sausage, onion, and garlic till meat is browned and onion is tender; drain off fat. Add *undrained* beans and remaining ingredients. Turn into a 1½-quart casserole. Bake, covered, in a 325° oven for 45 minutes. Uncover, bake 40 to 45 minutes more, stirring occasionally. Remove bay leaf. Serve in bowls. Serves 6.

Serves-a-Dozen Lasagna

1 pound bulk Italian sausage
½ cup chopped onion
½ cup chopped celery
½ cup chopped carrot
1 clove garlic, minced
1 16-ounce can tomatoes, cut up
1 6-ounce can tomato paste
1 teaspoon sugar
1 teaspoon dried oregano, crushed
½ teaspoon fennel seed
    Dash bottled hot pepper sauce
2 beaten eggs
2 cups ricotta cheese *or* cream-style
    cottage cheese
½ cup grated parmesan cheese
2 tablespoons snipped parsley
10 ounces lasagna noodles, cooked and
    drained
8 ounces mozzarella cheese, thinly sliced

In 10-inch skillet cook meat, onion, celery, carrot, and garlic till meat is lightly browned. Drain off fat. Stir in next 6 ingredients, 1 teaspoon *salt,* and ¼ teaspoon *pepper*. Cover; simmer about 20 minutes, stirring occasionally. Combine eggs, ricotta, parmesan, parsley, and ¼ teaspoon *pepper*. Place *half* the noodles in a greased 13x9x2-inch baking dish. Spread with *half* the cheese filling; top with mozzarella and *half* the meat sauce. Repeat layers of noodles, cheese filling, and meat sauce. Bake in 375° oven about 40 minutes. Let stand 10 minutes. Cut into squares. Makes 12 servings.

Sausage and Corn Bread

Combine sausage and a tomato-chili pepper mixture. Bake the sausage mixture between layers of corn bread. Then spoon the rest of the tomato mixture over squares of the corn bread –

1 16-ounce can stewed tomatoes, cut up
1 4-ounce can green chili peppers, rinsed, seeded, and chopped
1 teaspoon minced dried onion
½ teaspoon sugar
   Dash garlic powder
3 tablespoons cold water
1 tablespoon cornstarch
1 pound bulk pork sausage
¾ cup all-purpose flour
¾ cup yellow cornmeal
2 tablespoons sugar
1 tablespoon baking powder
½ teaspoon salt
2 beaten eggs
1 8½-ounce can cream-style corn
½ cup milk
3 tablespoons cooking oil

In saucepan combine the *undrained* tomatoes, chopped chili peppers, minced dried onion, the ½ teaspoon sugar, and the garlic powder; bring to boiling. Blend cold water into cornstarch; stir into tomato mixture. Cook and stir till mixture is thickened and bubbly. Remove from heat and set the mixture aside.

In skillet cook sausage till browned, stirring occasionally to break meat into bits and to brown evenly. Drain off fat. Stir *half* of the tomato mixture into the sausage; set aside.

In mixing bowl stir together flour, cornmeal, the 2 tablespoons sugar, the baking powder, and salt. In another bowl combine eggs, cream-style corn, milk, and cooking oil; add to cornmeal mixture. Stir just till moistened. Spread *half* the batter in a greased 9x9x2-inch baking pan. Spoon sausage mixture atop. Spread remaining batter over meat. Bake in a 375° oven about 30 minutes. Let stand 5 minutes. Cut into squares. Heat remaining tomato mixture and spoon over corn bread squares. Makes 6 servings.

Sausage Quiche

   Pastry for Single-Crust Pie
½ pound bulk pork sausage
¾ cup sliced fresh mushrooms
¼ cup chopped onion
¼ cup chopped green pepper
1 clove garlic, minced
3 beaten eggs
1½ cups light cream *or* milk
1 tablespoon all-purpose flour
¼ teaspoon salt
   Dash pepper
¾ cup shredded mozzarella cheese
¼ cup grated parmesan cheese
1 tablespoon snipped parsley

Prepare pastry. On floured surface roll out pastry till dough is about ⅛ inch thick. Line a 9-inch pie plate or quiche dish. Trim pastry to ½ inch beyond edge of pie plate. Flute edge of pastry high; do not prick. Line pastry with double thickness heavy-duty foil. Bake in a 450° oven for 5 minutes. Carefully remove the foil. Bake 5 to 7 minutes more or till pastry is golden. Remove from oven; reduce oven temperature to 325°. (Pie shell should still be hot when filling is added; do not partially bake it ahead of time.)

Meanwhile, in skillet cook sausage till meat is browned. Drain thoroughly, reserving 1 tablespoon drippings. Set sausage aside. In same skillet cook mushrooms, onion, green pepper, and garlic in reserved drippings till onion is tender but not brown. Remove from heat; set aside.

In bowl thoroughly stir together the eggs, light cream or milk, flour, salt, and pepper. Sprinkle sausage over bottom of warm pastry. Top with mushroom mixture. Place on rack in oven; gently pour egg mixture over mushroom mixture. Sprinkle with mozzarella cheese; top with parmesan cheese and parsley.

Bake in 325° oven for 45 to 50 minutes or till almost set in center. If necessary, cover edge of crust using foil to prevent overbrowning. Let stand 10 minutes before serving. Makes 6 servings.

Pastry for Single-Crust Pie: In medium mixing bowl stir together 1¼ cups all-purpose *flour* and ½ teaspoon *salt*. Cut in ⅓ cup *shortening or lard* till pieces are the size of small peas. Using 3 to 4 tablespoons *cold water,* sprinkle 1 tablespoon water over part of mixture; gently toss with a fork. Push to side of bowl. Repeat till all is moistened. Form dough into a ball.

Use a pie plate or quiche dish for baking Sausage Quiche. It's full of meat, vegetables, and cheese in a custard mixture.

Sausage-Macaroni Skillet

    1 cup medium shell macaroni
    1 pound bulk Italian sausage
    ½ cup chopped green pepper
    1 16-ounce can tomatoes, cut up
    1 10-ounce can pizza sauce
    2 cups thinly sliced zucchini
    1 cup shredded mozzarella cheese

Cook macaroni according to package directions; drain, rinse, and set aside. In skillet cook sausage and green pepper till sausage is browned and pepper is tender; stir occasionally to break sausage into bits and to brown evenly. Drain off fat. Stir in *undrained* tomatoes, pizza sauce, and ¼ teaspoon *salt;* bring to boiling. Stir in zucchini; cover and cook about 10 minutes or till zucchini is tender. Stir in cooked macaroni. Cook, uncovered, about 5 minutes more. Sprinkle with mozzarella cheese. Serves 6.

Sausage-Filled Crepes

   16 Crepes (see recipe, page 59)
    1 pound bulk pork sausage
    ¼ cup sliced green onion
    ¼ cup finely chopped celery
    3 tablespoons all-purpose flour
    ¾ cup milk
    1 3-ounce can sliced mushrooms
    2 teaspoons instant beef bouillon
       granules
    1 teaspoon worcestershire sauce
    1 cup dairy sour cream
       Snipped parsley *or* chives

Prepare Crepes; set aside. In skillet cook sausage, green onion, and celery till meat is browned and vegetables are tender; stir occasionally to break sausage into bits and to brown evenly. Drain off fat. Stir in *1 tablespoon* of the flour. Stir in milk, *undrained* mushrooms, bouillon granules, and worcestershire sauce. Cook and stir till thickened and bubbly. Stir together ½ *cup* of the sour cream and remaining 2 tablespoons flour. Stir into sausage mixture. Cook and stir till thickened and bubbly. Spoon about ¼ *cup* of the sausage mixture along center of unbrowned side of each crepe. Fold two opposite edges so they overlap atop filling. Place seam side down in 13x9x2-inch baking dish. Repeat with remaining crepes. Cover; bake in a 375° oven about 20 minutes or till heated through. Garnish with remaining sour cream and parsley or chives. Makes 6 to 8 servings.

Pan Pizza

   2½ to 3 cups all-purpose flour
    1 package active dry yeast
    1 teaspoon salt
    1 cup warm water (110°)
    2 tablespoons cooking oil
       Tomato Sauce
    1 pound bulk Italian sausage *or* ground
       pork, cooked and drained, *or* 6
       ounces sliced pepperoni, *or* 2 cups
       chopped Canadian-style bacon
       Sliced or chopped green onions, green
       pepper, mushrooms, olives, *and/or*
       canned green chili peppers
    2 to 3 cups shredded mozzarella,
       monterey jack, *or* Swiss cheese

For the crust (see Note) in large mixer bowl combine *1½ cups* of the flour, the yeast, and salt. Add warm water and oil. Beat at low speed of electric mixer for ½ minute, scraping bowl. Beat 3 minutes at high speed. By hand stir in enough of the remaining flour to make a moderately stiff dough. Cover and let rest 10 minutes.

On floured surface knead dough till smooth, about 3 to 5 minutes. Place in greased bowl; turn once and cover. Let rise till double, about 1 hour. Meanwhile, prepare Tomato Sauce; cool to room temperature before using.

With greased fingers pat dough out onto bottom and halfway up sides of greased 15x10x1-inch baking pan. Let rise till double, about 30 to 45 minutes. (Crust may be baked immediately after patting into pan, omitting the second rising, if desired.) Bake in 375° oven for 20 to 25 minutes or till deep golden brown.

Spread Tomato Sauce over hot crust. Sprinkle meat, vegetables, and cheese atop. Return to 375° oven and bake 20 to 25 minutes more or till bubbly. Let stand 5 minutes before cutting.

Tomato Sauce: Combine one 8-ounce can *tomato sauce;* one 7½-ounce can *tomatoes,* cut up; 1 medium *onion,* chopped (½ cup); 2 cloves *garlic,* minced; 1 tablespoon dried *oregano,* crushed; 1 tablespoon dried *basil,* crushed; 1 teaspoon *sugar;* ½ teaspoon *salt;* and ⅛ teaspoon *pepper.* Bring to boiling. Reduce heat; cover and simmer about 5 to 10 minutes or till onion is tender. Cool.

Note: If desired, prepare crust using one 13¾-ounce package *hot roll mix* instead of flour, yeast, and salt. Soften yeast from roll mix in 1 cup warm water (110°). Stir in flour mixture from the mix; omit the cooking oil. Cover and let rest 10 minutes. Continue preparation as above *except* do not knead or let dough rise.

Dry and Semi-Dry Sausages

Salami Bagelwiches

Choose from the many types of salami, such as cotto, German, and Italian varieties –

- 4 bagels, split and toasted
- 2 tablespoons butter *or* margarine
- 2 hard-cooked eggs, finely chopped
- 2 tablespoons mayonnaise *or* salad dressing
- 1 tablespoon finely chopped onion
- 2 teaspoons sesame seed, toasted
- 4 ounces Genoa salami, thinly sliced
- 3 ounces sliced Swiss cheese
- ½ medium cucumber, thinly sliced

Spread toasted surface of bagels with butter or margarine. In small bowl combine chopped eggs, mayonnaise or salad dressing, chopped onion, and sesame seed. For each sandwich, spread *2 teaspoons* of the egg mixture on one half of bagel; place ¼ of the salami, Swiss cheese, and cucumber slices atop. Spread 2 teaspoons egg mixture on cut side of remaining bagel half; place over other half. Makes 4 sandwiches.

Salami-Cabbage Skillet

- 2 slices bacon
- ⅓ cup packed brown sugar
- ⅓ cup vinegar
- ¼ cup water
- 1 teaspoon salt
- ½ teaspoon caraway seed
  Dash pepper
- 6 cups shredded cabbage
- 2 medium cooking apples, peeled, cored, and coarsely chopped (2 cups)
- 8 ounces sliced salami, cut into 2-inch strips (2 cups)

In 12-inch skillet cook bacon till crisp. Remove bacon; crumble and set aside, reserving drippings. Add brown sugar, vinegar, water, salt, caraway, and pepper to bacon drippings in skillet; bring to boiling. Add cabbage and chopped apple, stirring to coat. Cover and cook over low heat for 25 to 30 minutes; stir occasionally. Stir in crumbled bacon and salami. Cook, covered, 5 minutes more. Drain off excess liquid, if desired. Makes 4 servings.

Popover Pizza

The crust is on top for this pizza! If you like, you can use New England sausage instead –

- 12 ounces mortadella, cubed
- 1 medium onion, chopped (½ cup)
- 1 tablespoon butter *or* margarine
- 1 15½-ounce can meatless spaghetti sauce
- ½ teaspoon fennel seed
- 1 6-ounce package mozzarella cheese, thinly sliced
- 2 eggs
- 1 cup milk
- 1 tablespoon cooking oil
- 1 cup all-purpose flour
- ½ teaspoon salt
- ¼ cup grated parmesan cheese

In skillet cook mortadella and onion in butter or margarine till onion is tender but not brown; drain. Stir in spaghetti sauce and fennel seed. Pour mixture into ungreased 13x9x2-inch baking pan. Arrange sliced mozzarella cheese over top. In bowl combine eggs, milk, and cooking oil; add flour and salt. Beat with rotary beater till smooth. Pour batter evenly over cheese in pan. Sprinkle parmesan atop. Bake in 400° oven for about 30 minutes or till crust is golden. Cut into squares. Serve hot. Makes 6 servings.

Bologna-Bean Bunwiches

- 8 hard rolls
- 1 16-ounce can baked beans
- ½ cup chili sauce
- ¼ cup finely chopped celery
- 1 tablespoon minced dried onion
- 1 teaspoon worcestershire sauce
- ½ teaspoon chili powder
- 8 ounces bologna, cut into bite-size strips (2 cups)
  Shredded lettuce
- 1 cup shredded American cheese (4 ounces)

Split rolls; hollow out bottoms and tops, leaving edges about ½ inch thick. Set rolls aside. In saucepan combine baked beans, chili sauce, celery, onion, worcestershire sauce, and chili powder. Bring to boiling. Reduce heat; cover and simmer 5 minutes. Stir in bologna strips; heat through. Spoon bologna mixture into hollowed-out bottoms of rolls. Sprinkle each with shredded lettuce and shredded cheese. Cover with roll tops. Makes 8 servings.

Prepare easy-to-assemble Sausage Supper Salad using one or more dry and semi-dry sausages.

Sausage Supper Salad

    4 cups torn lettuce
    8 ounces assorted dry and semi-dry
         sausages (salami, cervelat,
         pepperoni, mortadella)
    ½ of a 15-ounce can (1 cup) garbanzo
         beans, drained
    1 cup sliced celery
    ½ cup chopped onion
    2 hard-cooked eggs, cut into wedges
    ½ cup mayonnaise *or* salad dressing
    2 tablespoons milk
 1½ teaspoons prepared horseradish
    ½ teaspoon dry mustard

Place lettuce in a large bowl. Cut meats into thin slices, then into bite-size pieces. Arrange meats, beans, celery, onion, and egg wedges atop lettuce. Blend together mayonnaise or salad dressing, milk, horseradish, and mustard; dollop in center of salad. To serve, toss mayonnaise mixture and vegetables and meat. Serves 4 to 6.

Beerwurst Soup

    1 cup chopped celery
    1 medium onion, chopped (½ cup)
    2 tablespoons butter *or* margarine
    1 tablespoon cornstarch
    ½ teaspoon dry mustard
    ¼ teaspoon garlic powder
    ¼ teaspoon dried oregano, crushed
    ¼ teaspoon dried basil, crushed
    ¼ teaspoon dried thyme, crushed
    1 12-ounce can (1½ cups) beer
    1 10½-ounce can condensed beef broth
    4 slices French bread
    1 cup shredded mozzarella cheese
         (4 ounces)
 12 ounces beerwurst (beer salami), thinly
         sliced and quartered

In large skillet cook celery and onion in butter or margarine till tender but not brown. Blend in cornstarch, dry mustard, garlic powder, oregano, basil, and thyme; add beer and beef broth. Cook and stir till thickened and bubbly. Cover and simmer over low heat for 30 minutes, stirring occasionally. Meanwhile, arrange bread slices on a baking sheet; sprinkle cheese atop. Broil 3 inches from heat for 3 minutes or till cheese is melted and lightly browned. Add the beerwurst to soup; simmer 2 to 3 minutes to heat through. Top individual servings with a hot bread slice. Makes 4 servings.

Cervelat Bean Salad

    ¼ cup olive *or* cooking oil
    ¼ cup white wine vinegar
    ½ teaspoon salt
    ½ teaspoon dry mustard
    ⅛ teaspoon pepper
    6 cups torn fresh spinach leaves
    1 15-ounce can garbanzo beans, drained
    1 Bermuda onion, sliced and separated
         into rings (1 cup)
    1 hard-cooked egg, sliced
    8 ounces cervelat, cut into strips

For dressing combine oil, vinegar, salt, mustard, and pepper in screw-top jar; cover and shake well. Chill. Place spinach leaves in large bowl. Arrange garbanzo beans, onion rings, egg slices, and cervelat strips in layers atop spinach. Just before serving, shake dressing and drizzle over salad; toss salad. Makes 4 to 6 servings.

Braunschweiger Pâté

    2 slices bacon
    1 pound braunschweiger
    1 8-ounce package cream cheese, softened
    2 tablespoons dry white wine
    ⅛ teaspoon garlic powder
    ⅛ teaspoon bottled hot pepper sauce
    ¼ cup finely chopped onion
    1 tablespoon milk
         Finely snipped parsley (optional)
         Assorted crackers

In skillet cook bacon till crisp; drain well on paper toweling. Crumble bacon and set aside. In mixer bowl combine braunschweiger, *half* of the cream cheese, the wine, garlic powder, and hot pepper sauce; beat with an electric mixer till blended. Stir in crumbled bacon and chopped onion. Chill 1 hour. Form into an igloo shape on serving plate. Combine the remaining cream cheese and milk; beat till smooth. Spread over the braunschweiger mixture; chill well. Sprinkle with parsley, if desired. Serve with assorted crackers. Makes about 2⅔ cups spread.

Sauces, Glazes, and Marinades

Quick Raisin Sauce

- ½ cup packed brown sugar
- ½ teaspoon dry mustard
- ¼ teaspoon ground ginger
- 1 22-ounce can raisin pie filling
- 2 tablespoons lemon juice
- 2 tablespoons water

In saucepan combine brown sugar, mustard, and ginger. Blend in raisin pie filling, lemon juice, and water. Cover and simmer for 5 minutes. Serve with pork or ham. Makes 2½ cups sauce.

Cumberland Sauce

- ½ teaspoon finely shredded orange peel
- ⅔ cup orange juice
- ½ cup currant jelly
- 3 tablespoons sweet red wine
- ¼ teaspoon ground ginger
- 1 tablespoon cold water
- 4 teaspoons cornstarch
- 1 tablespoon lemon juice

In saucepan combine orange peel, orange juice, jelly, wine, and ginger. Heat till jelly melts, stirring occasionally. Blend water into cornstarch; add to mixture in saucepan. Cook and stir till mixture is thickened and bubbly. Add lemon juice; cook 1 to 2 minutes more. Serve hot or cold with pork or ham. Makes 1 cup.

Texas Barbecue Sauce

- 1 cup tomato juice
- ¼ cup vinegar
- ¼ cup catsup
- ¼ cup worcestershire sauce
- 2 tablespoons brown sugar
- 2 tablespoons paprika
- 2 teaspoons dry mustard
- 1½ teaspoons onion salt
- ½ teaspoon pepper
  Several dashes bottled hot pepper sauce

In a small saucepan combine tomato juice, vinegar, catsup, worcestershire sauce, brown sugar, paprika, mustard, onion salt, pepper, and hot pepper sauce. Cover and simmer for 5 minutes. Brush on pork ribs, pork, ham, or sausage patties, or Canadian bacon slices. Makes about 2 cups sauce.

Onion-Mustard Sauce

A creamy sauce with a delightful tang –

- ⅓ cup milk
- 2 tablespoons regular onion soup mix
- 1 cup dairy sour cream
- 3 tablespoons prepared mustard

In small saucepan combine milk and dry onion soup mix; let stand 5 minutes. Stir in sour cream and prepared mustard. Stir over low heat just till heated through but *do not boil*. Serve warm sauce with pork or ham. Makes 1⅓ cups sauce.

Curried Cranberry Glaze

Pass any extra glaze with the cooked meat –

- ½ cup chopped onion
- 4 teaspoons curry powder
- ¼ cup butter *or* margarine
- 1 16-ounce can whole cranberry sauce
- 2 tablespoons light corn syrup

Cook onion and curry powder in butter or margarine till onion is tender but not brown. Stir in cranberry sauce and corn syrup; heat through. Spoon some of the mixture over fresh or smoked pork roast or ham during the last 20 to 30 minutes of cooking time. Reheat remaining mixture and pass with meat. (Or, spoon over cooked pork, ham, or sausage patties.) Makes about 1¾ cups cranberry glaze.

Spicy Strawberry Glaze

An easy glaze to prepare –

- ½ cup strawberry preserves
- 2 tablespoons lemon juice
- ⅛ teaspoon ground cinnamon
- ⅛ teaspoon ground cloves

In small saucepan combine strawberry preserves, lemon juice, cinnamon, and cloves. Cook and stir till mixture is heated through. Spoon over fresh or smoked pork roast or ham during last 20 to 30 minutes of cooking time. Makes about ⅔ cup.

Peppy Lemon Marinade

⅓ cup cooking oil
⅓ cup vinegar
1 teaspoon finely shredded lemon *or* lime peel
¼ cup lemon *or* lime juice
1 tablespoon worcestershire sauce
1 teaspoon dried marjoram, crushed
½ teaspoon garlic powder
½ teaspoon dry mustard
¼ teaspoon freshly ground pepper
   Several drops bottled hot pepper sauce
   Pork roast (about 2 pounds)

In a bowl combine cooking oil, vinegar, lemon or lime peel, lemon or lime juice, worcestershire sauce, marjoram, garlic powder, dry mustard, pepper, and bottled hot pepper sauce. Place meat in a plastic bag and set in a deep bowl or put meat in a shallow baking dish. Pour marinade mixture over meat. Close bag or cover dish; refrigerate 4 to 6 hours or overnight. Turn the bag or spoon the marinade over the meat occasionally to distribute marinade. Remove meat from marinade and roast according to chart on page 9; brush frequently with the marinade. Makes 1 cup.

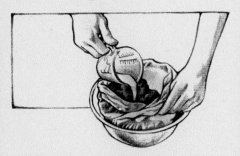

Marinating Meat

Use a plastic bag when marinating meat. The bag not only makes cleanup easier, but also makes it easier to distribute the marinade. Place the roast or meat pieces in the bag and set it in a deep bowl before pouring in the marinade mixture. Close the bag and turn to distribute the marinade over the meat. Turn the bag occasionally during the marinating period to evenly distribute the marinade mixture over the meat.

All-Purpose Marinade

⅓ cup wine vinegar
¼ cup catsup
2 tablespoons cooking oil
2 tablespoons soy sauce
1 tablespoon worcestershire sauce
½ teaspoon salt
½ teaspoon garlic salt
½ teaspoon dry mustard
¼ teaspoon pepper
   Pork roast (about 2 pounds)

In a bowl combine the wine vinegar, catsup, cooking oil, soy sauce, worcestershire sauce, salt, garlic salt, dry mustard, and pepper. Place meat in a plastic bag and set in a deep bowl or put meat in a shallow baking dish. Pour marinade over meat. Close bag or cover dish; refrigerate 4 to 6 hours or overnight. Turn the bag or spoon marinade over the meat to distribute marinade. Remove meat from marinade and roast according to the chart on page 9. Brush frequently with marinade during the last hour of roasting. Makes about ¾ cup.

Herbed Wine Marinade

½ cup dry white wine *or* burgundy
¼ cup chopped onion
¼ cup snipped parsley
¼ cup cooking oil
½ teaspoon salt
½ teaspoon dried thyme, crushed
½ teaspoon dried basil, crushed
¼ teaspoon dried tarragon, crushed
2 cloves garlic, minced
   Pork roast (about 2 pounds)

In a bowl combine white wine or burgundy, chopped onion, parsley, cooking oil, salt, thyme, basil, tarragon, and minced garlic. Place meat in a plastic bag and set in a deep bowl or put meat in a shallow baking dish. Pour marinade mixture over meat. Close bag or cover dish; refrigerate 4 to 6 hours or overnight. Turn the bag or spoon marinade over the meat occasionally to distribute marinade. Remove meat from marinade and roast according to chart on page 9. Brush frequently with the marinade during the last hour of roasting. Makes 1 cup.

Meat Guide

Buying Meat

When shopping for meat, the price you see on the label is the price per pound. If you are on a tight food budget, what you actually want to consider is the price per serving.

Some cuts of meat will give you more servings per pound than others because of less bone and fat. For example, a boneless piece of meat that is well trimmed of fat may have a higher price per pound than a roast with bone, but the boneless meat may cost less per serving because it has more edible meat. Use the chart at right as a guide to servings per pound when you are comparison shopping for cuts of pork and ham.

Storage

Proper care and storage will keep meat at its best by protecting against spoilage. Purchase meat that's sealed tightly and feels cold. Place in refrigerator or freezer as soon as possible. Consult the storage times at right for *maximum* storage. Follow label instructions for storage of canned products.

Fresh meat purchased precut and wrapped in clear flexible packaging may be refrigerated as purchased. If it's to be frozen, remove the clear packaging material and tightly wrap the meat in moisture-vaporproof freezer paper. The temperature of the refrigerator meat keeper should be between 36° and 40°F. Freezers should be 0°F or lower.

When working with meat, scrub cutting boards and utensils with hot, soapy water before and after each use. Diluted bleach also helps clean up cutting boards. Bacteria can be transmitted from unwashed cutting boards to meat.

Type of Meat	Servings Per Pound
Boneless meat (ground, cubes or pieces, Canadian-style bacon, boneless ham, pork sausage, variety meats)	4 or 5
Cuts with little bone or fat (chops, ham center slice)	3 or 4
Cuts with medium amount of bone or fat (bone-in ham or leg, loin roasts, bone-in shoulder arm picnic, boneless shoulder blade Boston roast, blade chops or steaks)	2 or 3
Cuts with much bone or fat (spareribs, country-style ribs, loin back ribs, hocks)	1 or 2

Besides the price per serving, other things you should consider when figuring how much meat to buy are: whether you plan to have leftovers from a particular cut of meat to use for another meal; other foods and their amounts you are going to serve with the meat; persons you will be serving (age, activity level, and appetite make a difference); and your refrigerator or freezer storage space.

Meat	Refrigerator (36° to 40°F)	Freezer (0° or lower)
Pork		
Roasts (fresh)	2 to 4 days	3 to 6 months
Chops, Spareribs (fresh)	2 to 4 days	3 to 6 months
Ground Pork	1 to 2 days	1 to 3 months
Whole Hams, Picnics (smoked)	7 days	2 months
Bacon	5 to 7 days	1 month
Cooked Pork	4 to 5 days	2 to 3 months

What Does Cooking Do?

Properly done, cooking improves the flavor and palatability of meat, and for less tender cuts also improves the tenderness. (Most pork cuts, however, are tender pieces of meat.) Two primary methods used to cook meats are dry-heat cooking and moist-heat cooking.

Dry-heat cooking methods, used for tender cuts of meat, include roasting (baking), broiling, grilling, panbroiling, and frying. Many fresh and smoked pork cuts are roasted or baked.

Moist-heat cooking methods include stewing, simmering, and braising. Moist heat is used not only for cooking less-tender cuts, but also for cooking some of the lean tender pork cuts. Some cuts of pork that are often braised include chops, ribs, tenderloin, and shoulder steaks. Those that are simmered in liquid include spareribs, fresh and smoked hocks, and country-style ham.

Generally, use low to moderate cooking temperatures for pork. Overcooking or cooking at too high a temperature increases the evaporation and loss of drippings.

Meat Cookery by Microwave

Microwave cooking works for most meat cuts (you may notice a difference in color and tenderness from conventionally prepared meat), and is great for heating ham. Besides cooking you can use the microwave oven to defrost meat and speed up barbecuing. Since microwave ovens vary with manufacturer, check your owner's manual for specific recommendations.

Meat Thermometers

Timings given in recipes and roasting charts are always approximations. No two ovens cook the same way and no two roasts are exactly alike. A meat thermometer is your best guide to judge the doneness of meat. For the most accurate thermometer reading, make sure the tip of the thermometer isn't resting on bone, fat, or the bottom of the pan. When the thermometer indicates the desired doneness, push it into the meat a little farther. If the temperature dips, leave roast in longer and check temperature again.

MEAT CARVING

Carving various pork cuts is not all that difficult if you have the proper equipment and know just where to make the cuts in the meat. To carve meat successfully keep the knife's cutting edge very

sharp. For best results, sharpen knives with a hand-held sharpening steel or stone before each use. With a steel or stone in one hand, hold knife in other hand at a 20° angle to sharpener. Draw blade edge over sharpener, using a motion that goes across and down at the same time. Turn blade over, reverse directions, and sharpen other side an equal number of times.

Keep knives clean. After each use, wash them with soapy water and dry thoroughly. Proper storage is essential to keep knives in good condition. Store knives either in a holder or in a rack to keep knives separated or to prevent them from being blunted. Knives will be more efficient for a longer period of time when handled with care.

Crown Roast

Remove stuffing from center. Or stuffing can be carved with meat. Use a fork to steady roast; start carving where ribs are tied. Cut between ribs; remove a chop at a time.

Shank Half of Ham

Place the shank of the ham at the carver's left; turn ham so the thick piece of meat is on

top. Steady ham using carving fork. Using a sharp knife, cut along the top of the bones (shank and leg) and under the fork as shown, loosening a boneless cushion. Remove the cushion and place cut side down on a cutting board.

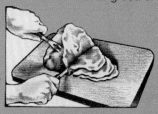

With the cushion piece of meat on a cutting board, cut perpendicular slices using a carving knife as shown. Use a fork to steady the meat as you slice. Transfer cut slices of meat to a serving platter.

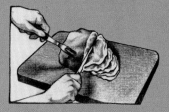

Use the tip of the knife to cut around the leg bone and remove any meat from the bone. Turn the meat so the broadest side is down as shown. Cut perpendicular slices in the same manner as for the boneless cushion piece. Transfer cut slices of meat to platter.

Rump Half of Ham

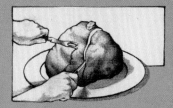

Place cut side of rump half of ham down on cutting board. Notice that on one side of

continued

ham there will be a boneless piece that can be cut away from the bone. Cut along bone from top to board as shown on page 91. The piece can be on either side of the bone, depending on whether ham is from left or right leg.

With the boneless piece of meat placed cut side down on the cutting board, slice meat across the grain as shown.

To carve the meat remaining on the bone, insert fork into meat next to bone and make horizontal slices to the aitch bone as shown. Cut away each slice from the bone using the tip of the knife and transfer cut slice to platter.

Whole Ham

Place the whole ham on a cutting board with the shank to the carver's right. Locate the kneecap. Cut away several lengthwise slices from the thin side of the leg that contains the kneecap, as shown. Use a fork to steady the meat.

Place ham on side where you removed slices. Make perpendicular slices to the leg bone, starting where shank and leg bones join.

To loosen slices, cut along leg bone as shown and remove.

Shoulder Arm Picnic

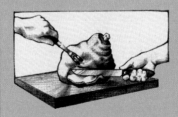

Follow these directions for a roasted fresh shoulder arm picnic or a smoked shoulder picnic. Remove a lengthwise slice from smaller side of roast as shown.

Place roast on side where you removed slices for base. Locate elbow bone and cut down to arm bone in front of elbow bone. Cut along arm bone.

Remove the boneless piece of meat and place it on a cutting board. Cut perpendicular slices from this boneless piece of meat as shown.

Remove boneless pieces from both sides of arm bone and cut into slices.

Pork Loin Roast

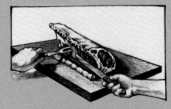

Before carving roast, cut away backbone piece, removing as little meat from roast as possible. Place roast on platter with largest side down and with rib side facing the carver.

Place fork in top of roast to steady meat. Cut along each rib as closely as possible. One slice will contain rib bone and the next slice will be a boneless piece of meat.

Index